D

Young Adult's

Guide

to the

Global

Workplace

Karen S. Hinds

New Books Publishing
Waterbury, Connecticut

YA

New Books Publishing
Waterbury, Connecticut

Hinds, Karen S.
A Young Adult's Guide to the Global Workplace

ISBN 0-9679861-5-X

Library of Congress Control
Number: 2011926824

Cover Design: Ed Tuttle
             Eklektos

Editing: Carolyn Quinto
         Blue Pencil Services

Cover Photograph: Raphael Edwards

ACKNOWLEDGEMENTS

Yvette Furlonge for your invaluable suggestions, professionalism and commitment to helping young adults excel personally and professionally; and Hajer Serag Eldin Shahin for your research and enthusiasm for the work we do.

To my students at Post University—Samantha Pagano, Laquasia Hailey, Brooke Fowler, Michael MacDonald, Sirdarius Johnson, Debbie Bertrand, Kayla Clarke, Nicole Pascarello, Kelsey Menard, Migdariana Mejias, Stephen Correia, Julie Wise, Larry Smith, Kimberly Benson—thank you.

To my Phase 2, Granville Academy students—Kyle Reid, Rachel Lamb, Dashayna Brown, Eric Respass, Camille Woods, Shalanda McCray, Joshua Singleton, Andrea Roscoe, Chad Taylor, Michelle Saunders—thank you.

Carolyn Quinto, thank you for pushing me to get this book done. I appreciate you. Thanks Robert Felder, Katie Zurlo and Judith Edwards.

Honor to God for my gifts of writing and speaking. Thank you to my family for allowing me to live each day as if it's my last day and my best day; my husband and son Shugas and Shugas Jr., my nieces Yanissa, Tianna, Keyondra, Breyondra —see, I did it! Thank you.

TABLE OF CONTENTS

CHAPTER 15: MANAGING CAREER LANDMINES

CHAPTER 16: TAPPING INTO YOUR ENTREPRENEURIAL TALENTS

CHAPTER 17: DOCUMENTING YOUR JOURNEY OF A THOUSAND MILES

PREFACE

If you can understand the basics of the workplace at an early age, there is no limit to what you can achieve in your career. I've made my share of mistakes building my career and always wish I had known more about the game of work much sooner.

Regardless of what part of the world you live in, we all have a desire to use the talents and gifts we've been given, but it's not enough to have that desire. It's very important that you understand the rules of the workplace so you can avoid costly career mistakes which can slow your professional growth.

You're probably reading this book because a teacher, parent, or the company you work for bought it for you. Some of you may have gotten it on your own. You're probably wondering, "What is it with all this work stuff? How hard could it be to show up, do what they say, and get paid?"

There are norms or unspoken rules that you are expected to live by when you go into the workplace. It does not matter if you are a cashier at a fast food restaurant or a new college graduate with a great new entry level job in marketing—the rules still apply.

You may ask, "How am I supposed to know these rules if they are unspoken?" This book will help you understand the unspoken rules of the work world and create a foundation for excellent work habits, success, and achievement in your future career.

v

ABOUT THE AUTHOR

Karen S. Hinds is a consultant, motivational speaker and Founder/CEO of Workplace Success Group. Workplace Success Group provides workforce development solutions to organizations committed to increasing the effectiveness of emerging talent.

The company partners with organizations to identify, develop and retain global emerging talent who are responsible, respectful, and results oriented.

This is accomplished by facilitating global events in colleges, universities and high schools, corporate training programs, monthly mentoring subscriptions and with books, DVDs and e-learning programs.

Karen is also the author of *Get Along, Get Ahead: 101 Courtesies for the New Workplace*; *Networking for a Better Position & More Profit*; and *A Teenager's Guide to the Workplace*.

She is from the beautiful Caribbean island of St. Vincent and the Grenadines and is a graduate of the Boston Public Schools and Bowdoin College in Brunswick, Maine. Karen lives in Connecticut with her husband and son.

www.workplacesuccess.com

CHAPTER ONE

UNDERSTANDING THE GAME OF WORK

- What Employers Really Want

- Fifteen Ways to Prepare for a Job Shadow Day

- Turning Your Internship Into a Full-Time Position

- Your First Job

- Ten Ways to Find a Job

Did you know?

Of the total U.S. population 25 years or older, 24% have a bachelor's degree or higher.

WHAT EMPLOYERS REALLY WANT

All employers want their employees to be successful. When you are hired, you are expected to perform and you get paid for your performance. There is no secret formula to being a good worker. You simply have to take the time to learn the basic expectations and then do your best to excel in those areas. What are some of the skills of good employees? If you work on developing the following, you are well on your way to becoming an exceptional worker.

Employers want someone who is...

- Computer literate
- Able to exceed the needs of customers
- Honest
- Able to listen and follow simple directions
- Willing to learn
- Able to get along with different people
- A problem solver
- A good communicator, written and verbally
- Responsible
- Respectful
- Flexible
- Loyal
- Confident
- A critical thinker
- Professionally attired according to company dress code
- A team player
- Able to manage time
- Pleasant and possesses a good attitude
- Creative
- Willing to go above and beyond what is required

FIFTEEN WAYS TO PREPARE FOR
A JOB SHADOW DAY

One of the best ways to learn more about a career is through a job shadow experience. You get to spend time with someone who is currently working in that career to observe what they do on a daily basis. Although many schools participate in district-wide job shadow days, you can also arrange your own even if you are working full time already. Here are a few tips to make your job shadow experience even more meaningful.

1. Sign up early. As soon as the opportunity to participate in a shadow comes along, be one of the first to say yes. This increases your chances of getting to shadow the professional of your choice.

2. Arrange your own job shadow. If your school does not offer a job shadow day, ask your parents, friends, neighbors, counselors, co-workers or religious leader for help in finding a professional to shadow.

3. Get contact information. If you arrange your own job shadow, make sure you have the name, address, department and phone number of your job shadow contact.

4. Prepare your résumé. Take an edited copy of your résumé with you.

5. Arrive on time. If you are going with your school, get to school on time to ride the bus. If you arranged it on your own, arrive 10-15 minutes before your appointed time.

6. Take a notebook and pen. You need to take notes as it shows your host that you are serious about learning.

7. Ask questions. Develop a list of at least 10 questions. Ask about a typical day, challenges of the job, specific skills, roles and responsibilities, personal characteristics, education and training required for the career.

8. Turn off cell phones. No texting, checking social media, or talking on the phone.

9. Be respectful. If you are in a large group, avoid extended conversations with friends. You are in someone else's workspace and your loud behavior can disturb the other workers and embarrass your school.

10. Dress appropriately. Different careers require different attire. If you are shadowing a maintenance person, your attire will be different than that of a student shadowing a businesswoman.

11. Don't go with your best friends. Chances are if you go with your best friends, you will spend more time talking to them instead of listening, learning and asking questions.

12. Use your manners. Address people as Mr. or Ms. during your job shadow unless you are given permission to use their first names.

13. Participate. Some job shadow hosts go out of their way to make the experience fun. Don't sit on the sidelines--get involved and participate in all the activities and have a positive attitude.

14. Say thank you. Make sure you verbally thank the people who took time to share their experiences with you.

15. Ask for business cards. Use the contact information on the business card to send a handwritten thank-you card to each person you shadow. You may send an initial email, but a handwritten note says you are a very classy person.

TURNING YOUR INTERNSHIP INTO A FULL-TIME POSITION

Internships are a great way to test drive a career. You get an insider's view into the day-to-day activities of the career to determine if you are passionate about it. Internships are also perfect résumé builders for college students as many companies expect you to have some experience in your desired field. The rapid decline of the economy in recent years has also made internships critical for seasoned professionals considering career changes or for those looking to land a new position.

Treat your internship as if it were a real job. Many companies hire interns as full-time employees if they've done a great job.

Talk with your supervisor and express your interest in working for the company. Ask for advice on the best way to make that happen.

Exhibit professional decorum by maintaining confidentiality and adhering to the company's dress code.

Volunteer for extra duties in your department and company wide; do them well. This gives you the opportunity to showcase your skills in a variety of settings and expand your network. Treat each task as if it's the most important task, even the grunt work. Everything has a purpose; learn how the small tasks fit into the big picture.

Search out mentors in the company who can guide you. A good mentor will help you to avoid common errors that can limit your career and increase your chances of reaching your goals.

Ask lots of questions and listen to the answers. The key is to observe and then analyze the information you receive to further enhance your ability to perform.

Be friendly to everyone you meet and introduce yourself to the people in your department. Quality connections with colleagues are the difference between a smart person who excels and one who does not.

Act as if you already have the job and always strive to be exceptional. People like to know what they are getting before they actually buy and the same thing is true in hiring. Let your employer see the quality of work you can produce and display your professional attitude. It will increase your chances of being asked to return.

Stay in touch with work colleagues and supervisors after your internship ends and build those relationships. Success is not only about what you know. You need good relationships with people who can help position you for promotions, tell you about open positions and guide you.

Be aware of the latest industry news. Stay abreast of changes and the latest developments relevant to your career and industry. This will help you to anticipate ways in which you can constantly upgrade your skills to remain employable and be a sought-after employee.

Connect with a Human Resources recruiter and inquire about potential opportunities in other business sectors. Skills developed in one sector are transferable to other business sectors.

YOUR FIRST JOB

The economic troubles of the last few years have made it even more difficult for young adult job seekers to find opportunities, but it's not impossible.

Whether you want to work full time in the summer or part time during the school year, it's important to know that you are gaining valuable work skills with each job regardless of the position. You are learning how to work with different people, how to conduct yourself in a professional work environment, and many other skills.

Your work experience will help boost your college applications, and for those students who choose to work right after high school, employers will consider your past work experience as an asset.

Your number one obligation, however, is getting an education, and your work hours should allow time in your schedule to complete school assignments.

It doesn't matter in what industry you find your first job because your emphasis should be on getting your foot in the door and taking the time to learn the game of work. Work has its own rules like any sport, and the quicker you understand the rules and practice, the faster you will rise.

TEN WAYS TO FIND A JOB

There are literally tons of resources that can help you find a job. Be patient—it will take some time. Your persistence and consistency will pay off. Here are a few tips to help you.

1. Talk to your friends who currently have jobs and find out where they work and how they got their jobs. Ask if their company is hiring.

2. Let everyone know that you are looking for a job.

3. Look through your local newspapers.

4. Walk around your neighborhood and downtown area and look for buildings with "help wanted" signs.

5. Ask your parents, siblings, and other family members to ask around among their friends to see who might be hiring.

6. Check out the online job boards. Many companies post job listings on their websites and on career sites like www.monster.com and www.careerbuilder.com.

7. Talk to your career counselor, teacher, or guidance counselor.

8. If you have a mentor, ask that person for help.

9. Go through your school's alumni network and conduct informational interviews with a few alumni and let them know you are looking.

10. Call your city's job hotline.

Finding a job is *your* responsibility. Don't sabotage your search by assuming others should know and will call you. Even though people are willing to help, it is up to you to remind them, pleasantly, that you are still looking. Remember, be patient, persistent, and consistent.

CHAPTER TWO

APPLYING FOR A JOB

- Creating a Résumé That Sells Your Skills

- Common Résumé Mistakes

- Sample Résumés

- Top 10 Cover Letter Mistakes You Don't Want To Make

- Cover Letter Format

- Preparing for a Job Interview

- Possible Interview Questions

- Telephone and Video Interviews

- Can You Speak on My Behalf? Using References

- Writing a Thank-You Note

- Interview Checklist

Did you know?

The sentence "The quick brown fox jumps over the lazy dog" uses every letter of the alphabet.

CREATING A RÉSUMÉ THAT SELLS YOUR SKILLS

One of the basic tools in your job search is a résumé. Although some companies only require a completed application, many others expect you to have a résumé as well. **A résumé is important.**

Basic Résumé Content
- Name, address, phone number and email address.
- Create a summary of your most valuable skills instead of listing your objective.
- List a history of your work experience. Include where you worked, for how long, and your responsibilities.
- List education, military service, community service, certificates, awards, languages spoken, and any other special skills.

Résumé Essentials
- Keep it to one page. Try different fonts or adjust the size of the font.
- Avoid fancy fonts. Use Times New Roman or Arial with a font size of 12 pt. On a Mac, Geneva works well and maybe a 10 pt is okay.
- Use bullet style instead of long paragraphs.
- Be sure the spelling, grammar, and punctuation are all correct.
- Use plain white paper.
- Keep it clean and straight. DO NOT FOLD.
- Choose a format that is easy to read.
- Use appropriate keywords to brag about your experience, accomplishments, challenges and solutions applied.

Digital Friendly Résumés

When submitting résumés online, formatting is often lost in transmission.
- Prepare résumé in Microsoft Word.
- Use Adobe or another PDF formatting program and create a PDF to preserve the layout.
- Use plain text when cutting and pasting your résumé into an online application.

Seven Things to Leave off a Résumé

Do not include the following if you are doing a résumé for a job based in the United States:
- Ethnicity
- Marital status
- Gender
- Age
- Weight
- Health status or photo
- Names, addresses, phone numbers of supervisors

Curriculum Vitae

In the United States, a curriculum vitae or CV is commonly used by professionals in academic and medical fields. A CV gives an overview of your life's accomplishments and can include select personal information. It is usually longer than a résumé and can run 2-3 pages for entry level candidates or even more for seasoned professionals.

In the United Kingdom and other parts of the world, the CV is more commonly used than a résumé.

COMMON RÉSUMÉ MISTAKES

Your Format

Common Mistakes
> Using Microsoft templates
> Fancy fonts
> Small margins
> Giving your résumé a title
> Inconsistent formatting (style, fonts, aligned headings)

Work History

Common Mistakes
> Simply giving list of duties
> Listing every single job you've held
> Listing phone numbers, addresses and names of supervisors
> Including experience from elementary school
> Exaggerating or lying about your experience
> Using the following phrases: Duties included, Responsibilities included, Responsible for

Volunteer Experience

Common Mistakes
> Omitting this section

Education

Common Mistakes
> Listing all the courses you've taken in college and every award won

Special Skills

Common Mistakes
>Listing English as a language in a country where English is the official language

References provided upon request

Common Mistakes
>Including this statement at the bottom of your résumé. This section is not commonly used anymore

Digital Friendly Format

Common Mistakes
>Omitting keywords
>Formatting with bullets, boxes or bold letters

Overall Mistakes

>Typos
>Illegible fonts
>Too much personal information
>Fancy paper
>Creative layouts
>2-page résumé with no substance
>One page with microscopic print
>Inconsistent punctuation and tense usage
>Inclusion of hyperlinks
>References to religious and political opinions
>Folding your résumé
>Smudged résumé from dirt, food, etc.

JOE SUMMER
23 Greenback Drive
Success Town, CT 01010
203-555-4444   JSummer@bmail.com

EDUCATION
BA in Business Administration   Expected 2013
Success College   Springville, CT

WORK EXPERIENCE
Grant, Hinds and Edwards   Sunnydale, CT
Intern   Sept 2010-Present
- Monitor legal procedures in-house
- Observe court trials in Hartford and other local jurisdictions with an experienced attorney
- Maintain court calendar
- Process client interviews, letters and telephone calls
- File documents with local courts

Win Designs   Springville, CT
Cashier   March 2011-Present
- Process all store purchases
- Calculate daily store revenue
- Assist customers in making clothing choices

Success Supermarket
Grocery Bagger   Summer 2010
- Bagged groceries
- Cleaned cash register stations
- Assisted customers and carried bags to car

SPECIAL SKILLS
Fluent in Chinese

MONIQUE FASHION   Monique@bmail.com
43 Runway Drive, Paristown, CT 01010   203-444-5555

EDUCATION
High School Diploma   Expected 2012
Model High   Fallville, CT

CPR Certification   March 2011
Camp Reach   Derby, CT

COMMUNITY SERVICE
Volunteer   Sept 2010-Present
The Homeless Project   Sunnytown, CT
- Read weekly to homeless children
- Help serve food to families in the shelter
- Organize toy drive and back-to-school supply campaigns during the holidays

EXTRACURRICULAR ACTIVITIES
Member of Debate Team 2009-2011
- Researched information to support presentation
- Built arguments with a team to present to panel of judges
- Presented arguments publicly to large crowds

SPECIAL SKILLS
Website-building skills

TOP 10 COVER LETTER MISTAKES YOU DON'T WANT TO MAKE

1. Incorrect title for the person to whom the letter is addressed; addressed to the wrong person or not personalized. Try to get the name of the HR contact or hiring manager. If that fails, then use "Dear Sir/Madam."

2. Asking the reader to refer back to your résumé: "As you can see on my résumé…"

3. Spelling and grammatical errors. Get a teacher, counselor or friend to help you review your letter and avoid errors.

4. Excluding your mailing address; omitting your signature. This shows your lack of attention to detail.

5. Too lengthy or too short. More than 2-3 short paragraphs is too much and a few lines will not cut it.

6. Lack of focus. Failure to hone in on key reasons to hire to you.

7. Giving a laundry list of attributes without evidence to back them up; e.g., "I am hard working, dedicated, customer oriented, and I believe I will be a good asset to the company" means nothing to the company.

8. Boring beginnings. "I am applying for the position of…" or " I saw your ad online" will not capture your reader. Add a short sentence that expresses your enthusiasm for the position or outlines your qualifications.

9. Getting ahead of yourself. Present yourself very confidently, but not boastfully, then let the decision maker do his job.

10. Avoid generic letters. Each letter should be personalized with the position and employer. Take the time to research the employer and demonstrate that in the letter as well.

COVER LETTER FORMAT

Your Name
Address
City, State, Zip Code

Date

Employer Contact Information
Name
Title
Company
Address
City, State, Zip Code

Greeting
Dear Mr. /Ms. Last Name,

First paragraph
Let the employer know why you are writing. If you were referred, mention the name of the person who referred you. Mention the position to which you are applying and add a sentence about why you are unique.

Second paragraph
State why you are uniquely qualified for the position.
Pick 2-3 key points from your experience to highlight. Do not restate résumé verbatim.

Third paragraph
Thank the employer, reiterate your interest in the position and state how you will follow up.

Closing
Sincerely or Best Regards,

Sign your name

Print your name

PREPARING FOR A JOB INTERVIEW

For your interview to be a success, there are a few essentials that must be attended to before you begin answering questions. The tips that follow will help you make the best impression before, during, and after the interview.

Before the Interview

1. Know how to get to the interview location. If the address is unfamiliar, take a trip to the general area a few days before the actual interview. Look for parking areas if you plan to drive or time your walking distance if you need to walk to the location or take public transportation.

2. Prepare a typed list of references and take three copies with you to the interview. Ask three people who know you well (such as teachers or counselors at school, a former employer, or your religious leader) if you can give their names as references. On your list, give their name, title (if any), their phone number, and how they know you. Do not EVER give a reference without asking for permission first!

3. Research the company. Find out general information about the company: what kind of business it is, who are their customers, does it provide a service or produce a product for sale? Check the library, website, or call the Chamber of Commerce.

The Day of the Interview

1. Take three copies of your résumé and three copies of your list of references. Make sure they are unfolded in a clean folder. Offer one of each at the beginning of the interview.

2. Go to the interview alone. Do not take a friend or relative or have anyone meet you after the interview within the interview area or the parking area. Meet or have them pick you up around the corner.

3. **Arrive on time.** It's okay to arrive about 5-10 minutes early, but NEVER arrive late. Arriving more than 10-15 minutes early can be an inconvenience to the interviewer.

4. **Dress for work.** Look professional, clean, and well groomed. Refer to the chapter on "Impression Management" for tips on personal grooming and dressing for the workplace.

During the Interview

1. Turn off your cell phone before entering the building. You want to make a good first impression and a ringing phone will not make you look important.

2. Remain calm and relaxed. You probably will be a little nervous but try to breathe slowly to help calm the butterflies.

3. Address the interviewers by name. Unless you are given permission to use a person's first name, be respectful and use a title (Mr. or Ms.) and last name when addressing them.

4. Avoid fidgeting. It's distracting and makes you appear less confident.

5. Answer questions honestly. Lying or exaggerating when answering questions will only reflect badly on your character, especially if your references say something different or if you are hired and the interviewer finds you out later.

6. Be brief and precise when answering questions. Providing lengthy answers, giving irrelevant information, or answering questions with one word ("yes" or "no") will not present a professional image of you. Instead say "No, I don't have any experience doing that" or "Yes, I can start on Monday."

7. Have at least three prepared questions. Feel free to ask your questions throughout the interview. The interviewer will probably ask you if you have any questions. Never say "No, I do not have any questions." Always come prepared with at least three questions to ask. Some examples might be: "What is the dress code for the job?", "What kind of training and orientation do you provide?" and "What do you think is the most important factor for me to do a good job for you?"

8. Ask for the interviewer's business card. If at the end of the interview the interviewer has not offered you a card, politely ask for one. "May I please have one of your cards?"

9. Ask about the time frame for making a decision. Ask the interviewer when he/she expects to make a final decision. This will help you to determine when to call and follow up.

1. Send a thank-you email. Within 24 hours of the interview, write an email saying thanks for taking the time to meet with you and include your contact information.

Note: Add a classy touch with a handwritten thank-you card after the email. Make sure your card is a plain blank card with just the words "thank you" on it. Please, no cards or email backgrounds with cute flowers, animals or poems.

2. Wait to hear from the interviewer. Be patient and wait to hear if you've been hired. Depending on what the interviewer told you their time frame was for making a decision, follow up shortly after with a polite email or phone call.

POSSIBLE INTERVIEW QUESTIONS

The interviewer will decide if you will be the best candidate for the job by the way you answer the interview questions. You should have a list of questions to ask the employer as well to make sure that this is the kind of company you want to work for. All employers want the people who work for them to be able to present themselves professionally and be reliable, responsible, honest, and hard working. These expectations are the same if you are filing in an office building or flipping burgers at the local fast food restaurant.

The following questions are typical interview questions. Look through these questions and think about how you would answer each one.

1. Tell me about yourself.

2. What are three strengths you possess?

3. What are three of your weaknesses?
This one is tough. Don't put yourself down. Instead of saying "I am always late getting work done," say (if it's true) "I am a perfectionist and sometimes need more time to complete the work."

4. Why do you want to work for this company?

5. Why should we hire you?

6. Why did you leave your last job?
This is a tough one, too. Never put down your former job or employer. Say something neutral such as "I want to try a different kind of work" or "It just wasn't something I felt I could be good at."

7. What are your dreams and goals?

8. What was the last book you read?

9. When can you start?

10. Do you have any questions for me?

TELEPHONE AND VIDEO INTERVIEWS

The internet has made the world of interviewing very exciting. Interviews are not just conducted in person anymore with many companies screening candidates over the phone and through video interviews. **All the rules of the job interview apply to the telephone and video interview.** However, there are a few other pieces you must take into consideration.

Phone Interviews

Dress up for the interview even though it is over the phone. It will put you in an interview state of mind. Stand or sit tall during the phone interview. It will help you to sound more confident.

Smile during the interview. Your smiles will be evident in your voice.

Put a little extra emphasis and enthusiasm in your voice. This is the major way in which you are being judged.

Record your voice and listen to the way you sound a few days before. You might be surprised, so spend some time practicing.

Quiet all background noises, siblings, pets, other phones, etc. Choose a quiet place where you will be uninterrupted.

Turn off call-waiting to avoid interruptions. Forgetting this will reflect badly on you and disturb your concentration.

Use a landline. This will reduce the possibility of a dropped call with your cell phone.

Video Interviews

Choose a neutral background. Take down questionable pictures from the walls and choose a well-lit location, preferably with a lighter color wall.

Sit at a clean table. It's fine if you have a bottle of water, pen, résumé and notepad on the table.

Sit still. Microphones tend to be sensitive so resist the urge to fidget or tap the table.

Do a dry run. Test your speakers and camera the day before and again 60 minutes before the interview. Use Skype to practice with a friend. It's a free video conference service available globally. **www.skype.com**

Show you are confident. Maintain eye contact with the interviewers by looking at the camera.

Dress your top and bottom. Don't be tempted to only dress up from the waist up for video interviews. This can prove to be embarrassing in the event you forget and stand during the interview.

Be punctual. If you are asked to report to a specific video conference center, arrive early so you have enough time to address any issues with the equipment.

CAN YOU SPEAK ON MY BEHALF?
USING REFERENCES

Who Qualifies to be a Reference?

- Former supervisors
- Clergy
- Guidance counselor
- Teachers/Professors
- Coaches
- Mentors
- Parole officers
- Someone who knows you well

Friends and family do not qualify unless you held legitimate positions or volunteered for them.

How to Get a Great Reference

- Ask permission before you include someone's name as a reference.

- Let the reference know who will be calling and approximately when.

- Make sure the reference is able to speak about your character and/or skills. Discuss the position and why you are qualified.

- Forward your résumé and any other information that will help your reference speak well of you.

MY REFERENCES

Reference 1

Name:_____

Address:_____

City:_____ State:_____ Zip:_____

Phone:_____Email:_____

Relationship:_____Years Known:_____

Reference 2

Name:_____

Address:_____

City:_____ State:_____ Zip:_____

Phone:_____Email:_____

Relationship:_____Years Known:_____

Reference 3

Name:_____

Address:_____

City:_____ State:_____ Zip:_____

Phone:_____Email:_____

Relationship:_____Years Known:_____

WRITING A THANK-YOU NOTE

Although saying thank you by email is quick and convenient, taking the time to send a handwritten note will demonstrate to the interviewer that you are serious about getting the position.

Buy the appropriate card. Use a card that just says "Thank You" on the outside and is blank inside. Stay away from cards with flowers, animals or cute drawings.

Practice your handwriting. The note needs to be handwritten so practice if you need to. Never use all capital letters.

Greet the person: Dear Mr. Smith or Dear Ms. Smith.

Say thank you. Take the time now to express your gratitude for the interview.

Remind them of why you are a good fit. Use this moment to briefly recap in one or two sentences why you are the best fit for the position.

Wrap it up. Express your enthusiasm for the position and the opportunity to work with the company.

Close your note. End using Sincerely or Best Regards to conclude.

Sign the note. Sign your name and then print it, especially if your signature is difficult to read.

Proofread your note. Spelling and grammatical errors will diminish the power of your note.

Send cards after each interview and to each person. If you had multiple interviews with multiple people, make sure to send a personalized card to each interviewer.

INTERVIEW CHECKLIST

Bring these to the interview:

- Three copies of your résumé
- Social Security card
- Green/Alien card (for legal immigrants to the U.S.)
- Two pens/two sharpened pencils
- Notebook
- Folder
- Directions to the location
- Name and number of the person/company contact
- List of references

Basic Professionalism in the Interview

- Dress for the job interview.
- Do not smoke or drink coffee right before the interview.
- Carry breath mints, not gum, and use right before the interview, not during.
- Be courteous and professional (please, thank you, calm tone of voice).
- Pack the confidence and a positive attitude.
- Watch the body language.

CHAPTER THREE

THE JOB IS YOURS, NOW WHAT?

- Evaluating Your Job Offer

- Twelve Things To Do the First Few Weeks on the Job

- Warning Signs of a Bad Job

- Decorating Your Workspace

- Nine Annoying Work Habits

Did you know?

Atlanta will create the most new jobs in the new millennium, more than 1.8 million by the year 2025, with Phoenix and Houston close behind.

EVALUATING YOUR JOB OFFER

Part-Time Employment

In your first job you will probably work part time and get paid minimum wage or a little bit above that, but take the job and get the experience. If you work for a clothing store or food establishment, you might get store discounts or free food.

Full-Time Employment

In addition to the financial gain, there are a few factors to examine before you say yes to a job offer.

1. Money. If you can't pay your bills with the money you will receive, think twice before saying yes. Check to make sure you are being paid what you are worth as the same job can have a different salary depending on the geographic location of the position. Is it 100% salary or partially commission? Will you get bonuses? How often will you be eligible for a raise? Is there a signing bonus?

2. Benefits and perks. How much vacation and sick time will you have? How many personal days? Are there gym memberships, tuition reimbursement, 401K, stock options, use of company car and cutting edge technology gadgets, concierge service, daycare services, etc.? Companies are all different in what they offer so ask for benefit information in writing.

3. Travel and schedule. Some jobs can range from no travel to 100% travel. The hours can be 9 a.m. to 5 p.m. or even 11 a.m. to 7 p.m. with no weekends or every weekend. Know what time schedule works best for you. Do you need flex time because of child care needs? These are all things to consider before saying yes.

4. The company and people. Consider the people you will work with. Do you feel like you will fit in? One lady turned a job down even though it seemed perfect until she met the supervisor and realized that the company politics and her supervisor's management style were not a match. There was no way their personalities would work well together.

5. Room for advancement. Sometimes a job offer may not offer bigger financial gains but it can position you to later move up in your career. You may move from one department to another because the new department has a direct route to the career you want. Make the move—every job change does not have to be a move up. Sometimes you may move across or even back and then up.

6. Put it in writing. Your offer should be in writing; keep a copy for your records. When you accept a new position, you should write and send a brief acceptance letter.

SO YOU HAVE MULTIPLE OFFERS

If you are considering multiple offers — Congratulations! You are in a unique position and a very good one.

1. Consider the options. Write out all the pros and cons of each position and each company and think about what will work best for you.

2. Don't rush your decision. If you need more time to make a decision, ask the company representative what the deadline is and request at least 24 hours to a few days.

3. Be honest. Do not lie about having multiple offers in the hope you will get hired by the company you like.

4. Negotiate. Some companies may be willing to match or even exceed another organization's offer. Don't just think about the financial gain.

5. Be polite and diplomatic. Thank the companies you reject and let them know that you have chosen another organization.

6. Stop looking for a job. Once you've accepted a position, you are now off the job market.

7. Don't flip-flop. When you accept a position, honor your word. Don't change your mind 24 hours later just because you were not sure.

TWELVE THINGS TO DO THE FIRST FEW WEEKS ON THE JOB

Starting a new job can be exciting and a little nerve-racking all at the same time. During those first few weeks, it is really important to make a positive impression on your boss and co-workers. Here's how you can do that.

1. Attend orientation. It might seem boring, but this is where you will learn the basics about your company and other critical information that directly affects your employment.

2. Recognize you have no job description. Don't expect to do only the things listed in your job description. If the request is not illegal or unsafe, get it done. Look at it as gaining new experience.

3. Ask lots of questions. You are still learning and no one expects you to know everything.

4. Set goals with your supervisor. Talk with your supervisor about what he/she expects and map out the projects and goals for your first few weeks or months.

5. Listen. You will learn so much more if you listen and learn.

6. Talk with your boss. This is not the time to be timid. Keep your boss up to date.

7. Keep a record. You should be tracking all your accomplishments, projects completed, etc. Your boss may not remember all you do, but you need to be aware of what you are learning for future reference.

8. Show up. This is the time to come in early and stay late. Build a good reputation for being respectful of time and resist the urge to leave work early.

9. Stay clear of gossip. It's easy to get sucked into company gossip. Avoid it.

10. Separate personal and professional business. Do not bring family or personal relationship drama to your job.

11. Have a great attitude. No one wants to work with a complainer. Be willing to help; smile and speak to as many people as you can.

12. Find a mentor and network. The first few weeks are the best time to meet new people and find a mentor.

WARNING SIGNS OF A BAD JOB

At some point in your life you will come across a really bad job. Hopefully you will see the warning signs beforehand and avoid it or get out as soon as you realize it. Some jobs just do not justify looking the other way, praying it improves or hoping for the best. In these instances, you simply need to devise a quick professional exit strategy.

So, what are some of the warning signs of a bad job?

You are asked to pay a fee. You should not be required to pay any fees to get hired. If you answer an ad online or in the papers and it asks for payment, there is a 100% chance it is a scam. Do not send any money to anyone to get a job.

Your paychecks bounce. If you cannot cash a paycheck, you have a serious problem—especially if it happens more than one time. You *need* to start looking for a new job immediately. Do not delay. Clean up the résumé and start hunting.

Your pay rate fluctuates without reason. When you were hired, you should have signed a contract that told you how much you would be paid and whether your earnings were salaried, commission based, or hourly. If your rate varies or goes down without proper explanation, you need to be careful that you are not being cheated. Be sure that you understand the reasons your rate changes, whether it goes up or down, and watch for consistency.

You are asked to be dishonest. Some companies cut corners. It could be watering down products, adjusting scales so they work in the company's favor, or cheating on time. If it is dishonest, it's only a matter of time before the scam is uncovered or it starts affecting you. This is another reason to polish up your résumé.

You are asked to pitch in financially. You really should not do this; however, if you decide to invest in the company with your own funds, make sure you know what you are getting yourself into. Draw up a legally binding investment document and be clear about the terms of repayment.

You have to furnish your own supplies. If your company expects you to provide your own office supplies in order to conduct office business, you should expect to be reimbursed.

You have no supervision or quality control. Last but not least, if you are not properly trained, if you are left alone with no supervision, if no one ever checks your work, or if you are not even sure you are doing your work well, beware. Likewise, if you rarely get to interact with anyone else in the company or if you are not even sure who else works for the company, it's time to look for a new job.

DECORATING YOUR WORKSPACE

You don't need to be an interior decorator to tastefully decorate your workspace. Because the majority of our day is spent at work, it's important to create a work environment that is comfortable and stimulating so productivity and creativity stays high. However, some people get so excited and territorial about their desk or office that they cross the line when decorating. Keep these tips in mind.

Your workspace is still company property. Make sure that the things you choose to make your space personal are limited but classy. If you have a collection, keep it small and confined to one place.

Keep your space tidy. There really is no such thing as an organized mess. Try to clear your workspace at the end of the day and maintain small neat piles if you thrive in organized chaos. If customers can see your work space, always have an uncluttered space so it is visually appealing.

Avoid inappropriate posters. Posters and calendars with buffed celebrities in swimsuits, in suggestive poses or with questionable sayings should be avoided. It's simply not appropriate for the office.

Limit family photos. Although it's important to have pictures of loved ones in your space, every inch of desk and wall space should not be occupied with family photos.

Keep clothing to a minimum and store discreetly. If you keep extra shoes or suits in your office, store in a closet or drawer and keep them out of sight.

NINE ANNOYING WORK HABITS

Sometimes it's the simple things that co-workers do that can test your patience. These habits can be so bad that they can change the mood of the co-workers and even slow down work. Other habits are simply inconsiderate. Are you guilty of these annoying habits?

1. Eating other people's food without permission. You probably brought your favorite lunch or the delicious leftovers from dinner only to discover that your lunch was missing when you went to the lunchroom. Eat only what you place in the office refrigerator.

2. Leaving the coffee pot or juice jug empty. If you drank the last cup or there are less than two cups remaining, take the time to refill the coffee pot or juice jug. Your co-workers will appreciate it.

3. Eating foods with strong odors in the work space. Food odors can be very distracting and long lasting so take your food into the kitchen or out of the building. That smoked herring smell will hang around for days.

4. Chewing gum noise. Avoid chewing gum at work. It is inappropriate, noisy, rude, and ugly to look at.

5. Using the last item in the supply closet. Notify the appropriate person if you used the last item from the supply closet. Reduce stress for the next person caused by the lack of small items like fax toner, ink cartridges, writing pads, and other supplies.

6. Permanent borrowing. You reach for the stapler and it's not there. Then you remember someone borrowed it but never returned it. Borrowing means you are allowed temporary use of an item. Return an item promptly or obtain your own.

7. Buffet manners. Buffets can be great but not if the person ahead of you is picking and touching the food. If you touch an item, it is yours. Look but do not pick through the items to make a selection.

8. Germ warfare. Some people insist on sharing their cold and flu germs. If you have a cold, wash your hands often and cover your nose and mouth when you sneeze. Clean your hand before you offer it in a handshake.

9. Hand washing in the bathroom. Restaurants especially post signs in the bathrooms asking employees to wash hands before returning to work. Do you?

CHAPTER FOUR

IMPRESSION MANAGEMENT

- What to Wear

- Appropriate Dress for Young Women

- Appropriate Dress for Young Men

- Casual Fridays

- The 411 on Accessories

- Taming Your Mane

- Ten Tips on Personal Grooming

- Dressing Your Personality for Success

Did you know?

A clothing item is considered vintage if it dates from 1920 to 1960. After that date, an item is considered to be retro, not vintage.

WHAT TO WEAR

Why should employers care about how you look as long as you get the work done? This is a common sentiment expressed by many young people. Let's look at it.

When your favorite sports team comes out on the field, they are dressed for the sport. Think of basketball, football, or soccer players: you never see any of them coming out onto the playing field or court in a tie and dress shoes, or a hockey player on the ice with a tank top and sneakers.

The same is true in the business world. Although many businesses do not wear uniforms and the technology industry has a more relaxed dress code, each workplace has a standard of dress that is expected in order to maintain a sense of professionalism, and if you plan to work in that environment, you need to follow the rules.

Some professional clothing can be expensive, but you do not need to spend a fortune to look professional and you do not have to buy brand-name clothing. Quality, moderately priced, professional clothing can be bought at a fraction of what some pay for designer clothing and sneakers. Check your local department store and compare prices.

When shopping for clothing, here are a few guidelines that can help you choose the most appropriate attire. The descriptions that follow assume you will be working in a work environment that prefers traditional work attire.

NOTE: If your job is of a physical nature, if you are working outdoors in dirty areas, or in retail, food service or health, your dress code may be different. Check with your company for policies on dress codes.

APPROPRIATE DRESS FOR YOUNG WOMEN

- Skirts. Should be no more than 2" above the knee.
  Choose material that does not cling to your body
  (e.g., spandex).

- Blouse or shirt. Go for a loose (not baggy) fit.
  Ensure that necklines do not expose any part of your
  cleavage.

- Jacket. A professional jacket flows past the waist area
  and ends mid-hip.

- Turtleneck. Should be worn under a sweater or jacket,
  not by itself.

- Sweaters. Some sweaters are appropriate if they are not
  close fitting, are not made with glittery material and are
  not studded with sparkles or fake jewels.

- Dress pants. Look for loose fitting (not baggy) pants that
  flow to the ankle. Make sure your pants do not drag on
  the floor. No jeans unless specifically permitted by
  the company.

- Scarves. Use to dress up your outfits.

Shoes for Women

- No stilettos
- 2" heels or shorter
- No dancer shoes
- Black, blue or brown for interviews

Clothing to Avoid for Young Women

- Tight jeans, skirts, sweaters, blouses, or dresses.

- Skirts or dresses with long slits that expose the thigh; slits should stop at the knee.

- Skirts made from light material where undergarment or body outline is easily recognizable.

- Midriffs, halters, or tank tops.

- Micro mini skirts.

APPROPRIATE DRESS FOR YOUNG MEN

- Dress shirt. Button down the front, long or short sleeves. Solid colors in a cotton or polyester with a collar so you can wear a tie.

- Dress pants. Khakis are often a good example of dress pants. Slacks or suit pants are, too. Pants should be worn on the waist with a belt. No jeans unless specifically permitted by the company.

- Dress shoes. Usually leather or leather looking and require a regular shine.

- Jackets. A sport coat or suit jacket is often optional for young men.

- Ties. Every young man should have at least three ties. Have fun when choosing ties and have at least one that is conservative.

- Turtlenecks. They are great under jackets or sweaters.

- Sweaters. Choose simple clean-cut designs without wild patterns or colors.

Clothing to Avoid for Young Men

- Lumberjack shirts.

- Muscle shirts.

- Baggy pants that fall below the waistline and drag on the floor.

• Exposed underwear.

• Baseball caps, du rags.

Clothing to Avoid for Both Men and Women

• Shorts
• Sneakers (depending on your job)
• Hiking boots
• Flip-flops
• Clothes with offensive language or images
• Fashionably torn clothing
• Sweatpants or sweatshirts
• Hats
• Shiny party clothing (glittery, neon, etc.)
• T-shirts
• Skinny pants

CASUAL FRIDAYS

Many companies have adopted a casual Friday policy. That does not mean you can now wear whatever you like. Workers who normally dress in suits all week are able to wear more relaxed attire such as a sport jacket with a turtleneck, button down or polo shirt. Women can dress down a bit without a formal business suit.

Since most young people do not dress in suits on a regular basis when they work, the clothing outlined in the previous pages is still the best on casual Fridays. Young men can probably choose not to wear a tie and clean jeans may be acceptable, preferably black and not ragged or patched. All items mentioned in the sections about clothing to avoid should still be excluded even on casual Fridays.

THE 411 ON ACCESSORIES

Your accessories are a demonstration of your sense of style. Earrings, body rings and beaded jewelry help make you different or a part of the crowd. However, a few tips can help you develop a new sense of style geared towards the workplace. It need not be for 24 hours a day, but it will help you look professional at work. Here are answers to commonly asked questions.

Q. How many earrings can I wear?
A. No more than two earrings.

Q. How many rings can I wear?
A. Keep rings to a minimum, 2 max.

Q. Why does it matter how many bracelets I wear?
A. They may not always see them, but chances are if you are wearing multiple bracelets they can hear them and it's distracting.

Q. Can I wear my rings and studs in other pierced body parts?
A. Not unless you are working in an environment where your accessories can actually help business, a body piercing shop for example.

Q. Why does the size of my jewelry matter?
A. Oversize pieces of jewelry are attention grabbers, especially large linked chains and flashy rings. You are in a job to work, not to be a fashion statement.

Q. Why can't I wear designer nails?
A. Nail shops have become creative with their designs, but long fancy designs with studs, tropical scenes, and loud colors are not appropriate for work. Wear a natural or soft-color nail polish. Short french tips are acceptable.

Q. Does the size of my purse matter?
A. Yes, it does. If you are going to an interview, women should carry a small or medium size purse. Bulky bags (especially shopping bags) or backpacks are too cumbersome and unprofessional.

Q. Why is the way I wear my makeup so important?
A. Some young ladies tend to overdo their makeup. Your makeup should be a soft way to enhance your natural beauty, not create a new you. Heavy foundation, bright or very dark-colored lipsticks, black outlined lips or eyes, too much blush, and extra dark eyebrows are some of the common makeup mistakes young women make when preparing for work.

Q. What about perfumes and aftershave?
A. None is preferred. If you insist, stick with light fragrances and wear in small doses. Many people have allergies to certain fragrances. Be sensitive to your co-workers' needs.

TAMING YOUR MANE

Your hairstyle is another way you express your sense of style. However, since your goal is to get a job and keep it, it's important to understand that this is another area where there are unspoken rules.

Young Women

1. Stay with natural human hair colors. Bright reds or varying shades of neon colors are not appropriate for a traditional work environment but might be okay for the music industry or if you wear hats all day long.

2. Avoid trendy hairstyles that are designed to be attention grabbers with spray-on glitters or spiked upwards or outward.

3. Extensions and weaves should be clean and neat at all times.

Young Men

1. Braids, dreads, ponytails and the no-comb hairstyles are not highly regarded in conservative workplaces.

2. Young men need to cut their hair regularly.

3. Low cuts are preferred.

4. Keep facial hair neat and trimmed (no designs, please).

TEN PERSONAL GROOMING TIPS

Here are a few personal grooming tips that will help you look polished and project a professional image.

1. Select your outfit the night before.

2. Check to make sure all outfits are clean, unstained, well pressed, have all the buttons and no split seams.

3. Make sure your shoes are comfortable.

4. Clean your shoes; no scuff marks.

5. Buy and carry with you an extra pair of pantyhose in case they run.

6. Shower daily and don't forget deodorant.

7. Clean and trim your nails.

8. No gum chewing. Freshen up with mints or breath strips.

9. Brush your teeth daily.

10. No smoking.

DRESSING YOUR PERSONALITY FOR SUCCESS

You are not totally dressed until you dress your personality. How do you dress your personality?

1. Have a positive attitude.

2. Smile.

3. Show enthusiasm.

4. Talk less, listen more.

5. Shake hands firmly.

6. Remember the names of people you meet.

7. Imagine positive outcomes.

8. Volunteer.

9. Make eye contact.

10. Treat others in a fair manner always.

CHAPTER FIVE

TIME IS MONEY

- Time Savers and Time Wasters

- On-the-Job Time Management

- Personal Time Management

- My Schedule

Did you know?

If you are an average American, in your whole life you will spend an average of 6 months waiting at a red light.

TIME SAVERS AND TIME WASTERS

Your life is busy. Time is spent at school, with family and friends, and at work. With such demands, good choices must be made about how your time is spent.

Time management is less about time itself and more about decision-making. Good decisions make it easier to manage your schedule and stay in control so you can maximize the 24 hours that we all have each day. When you make hasty or unplanned decisions, there are often unwanted consequences.

You are the one in control of your 24 hours and no one else. You get the credit for your choices. Likewise, if you choose not to accept that responsibility and use your time unwisely, you cannot blame others for the results.

Time Savers

- **Use a personal calendar**
It does not matter whether it's on your computer, in a smart phone, or in an appointment book. Record appointments, due dates for projects, and important commitments to help you stay in control.

- **Plan carefully**
Always estimate the amount of time a project or task will take to complete and then add in extra time for unforeseen circumstances that may cause delays.

- **Ask for help**
Smart people are the ones who recognize when they are unable to deliver by themselves and recruit others to assist.

- **Call ahead**

A quick phone call can save trips and time.

- **Set priorities**

Make choices and decisions based on your future goals rather than the spur of the moment.

Time Wasters

- **Worry**

More time is often spent worrying, stressing, and complaining about doing something than the actual time it will take to complete the task.

- **Over-committing yourself**

It's hard to say "no" when a friend needs your help. Your time is very valuable and it is unfair to yourself to spread yourself too thin and become overwhelmed by doing favors for others. Be selective and know when to say "no."

- **Chatting on the phone/texting**

Imagine sending 3,000 texts per month. In fact, texting has replaced talking on the phone for some people. As you text the days away, remember you also have a future coming up! Are you preparing for it?

- **Procrastination**

This behavior is best described as putting off doing something by any possible means or excuses. Stop sabotaging yourself.

- **Love sickness**

Hearts are being broken and hearts are falling in love all the time. A lot of time is spent preoccupied daydreaming about the other person. Keep an eye on your goals, too!

ON-THE-JOB TIME MANAGEMENT

One of the biggest differences between school and the workplace is the concept of time. In the work world everything seems to be measured by time. It's the old saying "time is money." With that in mind, there are a few points that most companies would like for all employees to understand. Mastering time management now will help you stand out as an exemplary student and employee. The following are common questions about time and the workplace.

Q. How can I be late for work if I'm in the building or in my work area?
A. The workday begins when you start working, not when you enter the building or the general work area. If you like to get refreshments before you begin to work, arrive early so you can get them and still begin on time.

Q. I have a legitimate excuse why I'm late for work--the train is always late and when I drive traffic is backed up. Why is my supervisor still making this a big deal?
A. Having an excuse for being late does not make everything okay. Part of the responsibility of being a good worker is to plan extra time into your travel schedule to accommodate unforeseen events when they occur so you can still arrive early.

Q. Why do I have to call if I'm only going to be a few minutes late?
A. It's the courteous, responsible thing to do. It lets your co-workers know how to reschedule their work if necessary.

Q. I call when I'm going to be late, but that does not seem to satisfy the people I work with. What should I do?

A. It's important that you call. However, when you are late other people in your department or on your shift may have to wait for you before starting their own work. If you are relieving someone, you are holding him or her up. Make an extra effort to arrive on time consistently so your co-workers may be more willing to understand when you do call.

Q. If I'm done with all my work, is it okay to leave a few minutes early?

A. No. It's great that you are able to complete all your work; however, you need to honor the time for which you are being paid. Do not start doing school assignments, personal business or ask your supervisor to leave early. Instead, ask for more work, assist a co-worker, or take the time to prepare for the next workday.

Q. I'm bored out of my mind and my supervisor is not giving me anything to do. She is always busy or not in the office. What should I do?

A. It can be frustrating if you have nothing to do and everyone else seems busy. Resist the urge to fall asleep or be unproductive. Approach your supervisor if that person is in the area or leave a note, email, or voice mail and let him/her know that you would like more work. In the meantime, check with co-workers to see whether you can help them. You will be showing that you are ambitious and not afraid to take the initiative to get the most out of your work experience.

Q. Is it okay to spend a few extra minutes at lunch, especially since other people in the department do it?
A. No, it is not okay. When you do that, you are cheating the company because you still expect them to pay you even though you are not working. You are laying the foundations and setting your personal standards for your future work life even if you feel your job now is insignificant.

Q. If I meet my friend during a quick run to the bathroom, why can't I stand and talk for a little while?
A. It's okay to meet fellow co-workers and friends during a break and exchange a few words, but it is not acceptable if you stop to have mini-marathon conversations when you are getting paid for working.

PERSONAL TIME MANAGEMENT

There are a couple of ways you can master your time. No, we are not asking you to be less spontaneous or to become rigid. Just take a few moments to plan your day so you accomplish the things you want. You will discover that what you make time for are the things you value the most.

Keeping a schedule is nearly impossible for some people. This can be made easier if you begin to identify the things that help you and those that hinder you.

Complete the following sentences:

What activities are your time wasters?

What can you do to save time?

When do you have the most energy to do school assignments?

How many hours can you work without feeling too tired or unable to complete other responsibilities?

How many hours do you spend weekly doing the following things?

      Extracurricular activities

      School assignments

      Watching T.V.

      Talking on the phone/texting

      Relaxing with friends

      Playing video games

      Working

What activities can you eliminate or reduce to gain more time during the day?

MY SCHEDULE

Start with a simple to-do list. Prioritize the things you need to do. Before deciding which items are high, medium or low priority, think about the consequences of not completing a task in a timely fashion.

High Priority - Must be taken care of immediately

Medium - Is important but can wait a bit

Low Priority - Things that have little importance overall

To Do's	Priority (H, M, L)	Completed (Y, N)

CHAPTER SIX

TELECOMMUNICATIONS

- Telephone Skills

- Fax Skills

- Internet for Business Use

- Social Networking Savvy

- What's the Big Deal About Sexting?

- Cyber Bullying

Did you know?

A recent survey of 500 top colleges found that 10% of admissions officers acknowledged looking at social networking sites such as Facebook to evaluate applicants. Thirty-eight percent of admissions officers said that what they saw negatively affected the applicant.

TELEPHONE SKILLS

Texting is more popular among young people than talking on the phone. In fact, some young people have not been taught how to use a phone for business purposes. Here are a few quick tips that will help you understand phone usage in the workplace.

- **Use the phone for business purposes only.**
Although some companies may not be concerned over an occasional personal call, it's best not to make personal calls on the company phone or on company time. Be aware that many companies do monitor their phone system.

- **Take proper phone messages.**
Most companies now have voice mail, but you may be asked to take a message manually. In such an event, make sure you have all the following information: name of the person who will receive the message, name of the caller, phone number of the caller, date and time of the message, the actual message, and your name and extension as the person taking the message. Remember to deliver the message.

- **Be voicemail friendly.**
When leaving a message, make sure to speak slowly and clearly, leave your name and phone number, and a good time to call you back.

- **No cell phones allowed.**
Company-issued cell phones are fine for the workplace. However, personal cell phones should be turned off during work hours. Check your messages during lunch or break periods.

- **Answer the phone professionally.**
Ask your supervisor about the preferred way to answer the phone. Most companies want you to identify yourself, the department and/or the company name.

- **Keep it clear, concise, and cheerful**.
Studies show that young people need to sleep more than the average person, but it's important not to sound sleepy when answering the phone; be cheerful even at 9 a.m. on a summer morning.

- **Ask before you hit the "hold" button.**
Saying "hold please" is not asking. Instead ask, "May I please put you on hold?" and wait for a reply before you put someone on hold. Then don't forget about the call on hold!

- **Learn to transfer calls.**
We've all lost a call trying to transfer it. Learn how to use your company's system so callers don't get lost in the phone system or fall deaf when you touch tone the numbers while they are on the line.

- **Pick up that ringing phone.**
If you are allowed to answer the phones, try to pick up the call by the third ring. Sometimes that may not be possible. However, it is best to strive for such excellence as the caller will appreciate your promptness and you will establish good habits for your future career.

FAX SKILLS

Although the fax machine is fast becoming obsolete, some countries still use it. When you are responsible for sending faxes or delivering incoming faxes to the appropriate recipients, here's how you can do a great job with this responsibility.

- **Always use a cover sheet.**
Fax cover sheets should be used with every fax and include the sender's name, fax and phone number; the recipient's name, phone and fax number; and the number of pages being sent. All companies have a standard fax cover sheet.

- **Learn to use the fax machine.**
Ask your supervisor or co-worker to show you how to use the fax machine correctly.

- **Ask for help when it's broken.**
Notify the appropriate person when the fax machine malfunctions. Do not be afraid; chances are it wasn't your fault and all that's needed could be minor maintenance.

INTERNET FOR BUSINESS USE

As enticing as the internet can be, it's best to think twice about using the internet or intranet in your workplace for personal email or activities. This includes using your smart phone to do internet lookups that are not related to work activities. Once again, you are being paid to do company work.

- **Use the internet for work purposes only.**
Resist the urge to update your Facebook status during work hours. Research should be work related, not for homework and school research papers.

- **Use proper English.**
Even though internet language has shortened phrases, please use proper English when sending emails to anyone in the company. Re-read your emails and do spelling and grammar checks before sending.

- **No chain letters.**
Do not forward chain letters, jokes or stories to co-workers. It is a time waster and clogs up other workers' email.

- **Know the rules**.
Typing emails in all CAPITAL LETTERS is considered rude and is equivalent to yelling. Sending unsolicited emails or spam is a violation of cyber rules.

- **Fill in the blanks**.
Complete the subject line in emails, give the proper salutations "Dear..." and remember to include your email signature (name, department, company, and phone number).

- **Avoid sending personal interoffice email.**
Don't email personal friends who work in the same company. Work is not the time to make plans with friends or find out how they are doing.

- **No instant messaging.**
Don't instant message friends while at work. You are on company time.

SOCIAL NETWORKING SAVVY

Social networking and social media have drastically changed the way we communicate. Although it's a great way to stay in touch with friends and family around the world, employers and colleges use the internet to discover information about job applicants and for potential college admission. One misstep online can cost you your college admission and even your job. Here are a few tips to keep your online profile clean and keep you safe.

FACEBOOK

Consider it first. Think twice before you post those photos that are racy and depict illegal or immoral acts.

Clean up. Delete posts from friends that contain offensive language and ask them to stop.

Check photos. Watch for photos where you are tagged and un-tag if necessary.

Don't advertise your location. Broadcasting on Facebook or Twitter where you will be or that you are going away is a recipe for disaster. This may attract predators who will take advantage of you or the fact that your home is temporarily unoccupied.

Think before you friend. Accepting a friend request from someone you do not know is dangerous.

Wait before you un-friend. Un-friending someone immediately after an offline fight is the equivalent of a friendship breakup. It is painful to some people and can cause problems offline so calm yourself before you make such decisions.

Leave it offline. If you have a fight with a friend, a disagreement with a boss, teacher or neighbor, or even problems at home, Facebook is not the place to discuss those matters. Keep them offline and resolve them privately.

Keep it private. There is no need to post your address, phone number or even your email address. Keep that information private. Don't post details about where you live.

Skip the gossip. As juicy as gossip can be, don't discuss other people in a public online space.

It's not a reality show. Posting in a negative way about your job, your boss or even a school that rejected you not only damages your reputation but it could mean legal troubles. Be careful.

Accentuate the positive. Facebook can be an invaluable tool to help you search for a job or internship and learn more about a college.

TWITTER

Much like Facebook, Twitter allows you to connect with people who are your followers. The same rules apply in terms of safety and tweet content.

www.twitter.com

BLOGS

If you keep a blog, it is not private even if just your close friends have the address. Everything you post is available publicly and is permanent.

www.Blogspot.com

YOUTUBE and VIMEO

These are video-sharing websites where users can upload, share and view user-generated video content such as personal home videos, TV clips, movies and music videos. Many people use YouTube and Vimeo as a video blogging site and attract a following of fans. Remember to keep your content clean.

www.Youtube.com   www.Vimeo.com

LINKEDIN

Although many of you may not have a LinkedIn profile yet, it's important to know about this professional network.

LinkedIn is strictly to make professional connections. Your updates should be professional.

Use a headshot only in your profile. This is the photo potential employers will see to help determine if you will fit into their organization so remove the earrings from any facial piercings you may have and tone down the makeup if you use heavy makeup.

Build a solid profile. Learn how to effectively build your profile with keywords and know how to use groups, answers and questions. Putting up your profile is not enough; you have to work the process to get your desired results.

www.Linkedin.com

WHAT'S THE BIG DEAL ABOUT SEXTING?

Sexting occurs when you send explicit sexual messages via instant messenger or cell phone.

So what's the big deal?

1. It is illegal under federal law in the United States to distribute or possess child pornography. Nude photos sent via electronic means classify as child pornography if the person in the photo is a minor. In some U.S. states, if convicted you may have to register as a sex offender for the rest of your life.

2. It never stays with just one person. No matter how much that friend promises not to share the message, it is almost always shared with at least one other person and can be widely distributed even if it was never meant to enter the workplace.

3. When racy pictures go public, some people may actually enjoy the spotlight; however, it can close many doors for you and even destroy your reputation for a long time.

4. Studies show teens girls are more likely to engage in sexting than boys.

5. If you are asked to send a compromising image, that person really doesn't care about you or your future. At the heart of sexting is lack of self-esteem and peer pressure, and it's time to deal with those self-esteem issues. Even if you feel confident and make a decision to take risky photos with your significant other, photos can still unintentionally leak out.

6. Sexting will never make another person like you more or even begin to like you.

7. It can damage your future chances of getting into college or your future career. Colleges and employers do search the internet for information on potential students and employees.

8. If you are involved in a sexting scandal, it will take time to rebuild some of the relationships that were damaged. Friends, family, neighbors and even co-workers will need to process the incident and deal with the feelings of embarrassment and humiliation they may experience. Give yourself the time to recover as well and things will improve.

9. Some people who find themselves caught up in sexting scandals may sink into a deep depression.

10. There is no safe way to sext. Think before you take that racy photo and hit the send button as there is no erase button. Once that image is online, it stays there forever.

CYBER BULLYING

Cyber bullying occurs when minors engage in targeted activities against another minor using the internet, cell phones or any technology.

According to the National Council on Crime Prevention, cyber bullying can be any of the following:

- Sending someone mean or threatening emails, instant messages, or text messages
- Excluding someone from an instant messenger buddy list or blocking their email for no reason
- Tricking someone into revealing personal or embarrassing information and sending it to others
- Breaking into someone's email or instant messenger account to send cruel or untrue messages while posing as that person
- Creating websites to make fun of another person such as a classmate or teacher
- Using websites to rate peers as prettiest, ugliest, etc.

The Effects of Cyber Bullying

In recent months the media has documented only a fraction of the negative effects of cyber-bullying attacks, and many minors do not report the problem. Unfortunately, too many attacks have resulted in suicide and suicide attempts.

Preventing Cyber Bullying

It can seem impossible to stop the barrage of cyber-bullying attacks once it's started, but there are steps you can take to stay safe.

1. As mentioned before, do not share your personal information.

2. Block the person or persons who are engaged.

3. Speak up and tell a trusted adult. You can also report the abuse online to www.wiredsafety.com.

4. Google your name and email address to see what comes up.

5. Take a break from the computer and do other activities. Go outside or spend time with your family.

6. Don't participate or encourage attacks on others.

7. Think before you send any emails or texts.

8. Ensure your emails and text messages are addressed to the right person.

9. Resist the urge to say anything that others could consider to be insulting, belittling or controversial.

10. Don't send emails and texts when you are angry.

CHAPTER SEVEN

NETWORKING

- Building Your Career Network

- Ten Informational Interview Questions

- Maintaining Your Business Contacts

- Finding a Mentor

- The Value of Volunteering

Did you know?

Body language specialists say that looking down is sometimes taken to mean that you have something to hide.

BUILDING YOUR CAREER NETWORK

One skill category that is important to develop is your networking skills. Networking with people is different than computer networking. Young people are already good networkers. Networking basically involves friends or business associates helping each other in their careers, hobbies or even personal matters.

This network of people is there to offer guidance to you as you make decisions that affect your life. Think of them as your very own group of wise people who are interested in your success.

You can choose a few family members, teachers, mentors, school friends, former supervisors and other people that you know. You want people you admire or people who are doing things you aspire to do.

When you connect with people, it's easier to find part-time jobs, get advice for life issues, advice about college and much more.

TEN INFORMATIONAL INTERVIEW QUESTIONS

A great way to build your professional network is through an informational interview. This is an interview where the goal is to get to know someone and their career. It is never asking for a job. Here are some questions you can ask in such an interview.

1. What were your favorite subjects in school?

2. Did you go to college; where and why did you choose that institution?

3. What was your college major?

4. Why did you choose your career?

5. Looking back on your life, what were the two biggest decisions you made that impacted your life?

6. What do you wish you could change about your professional career?

7. What decisions would you change as you look back on your high school/college career?

8. Have you made decisions in high school/college you regretted that affect your life now?

9. How did you handle challenges as a teenager/college student?

10. What advice would you give to a student now on how to succeed in life?

Think of at least two additional questions of your own.

MAINTAINING YOUR BUSINESS CONTACTS

It's important to stay in touch with your contacts. Don't wait until you need something to call or email. Here are a few ways to stay in touch.

1. Send birthday cards and holiday cards.

2. Send articles from the newspaper and web links that may interest this person.

3. Send them information on your successes, report cards, game schedules, etc.

4. Invite them out for a quick bite to eat when you both have time.

5. Ask their opinion on school projects or career decisions.

6. Seek referrals when job hunting.

7. Volunteer to help them on their projects.

8. Call or email occasionally just to say hello.

9. Create a LinkedIn profile and invite your professional connections into your network.

FINDING A MENTOR

You need a mentor. There is no rule that says you can have only one mentor. In fact, it will be to your advantage to have a few mentor relationships that can help you grow in different areas of your personal and professional life. Before you start your search for a mentor:

Be clear about why you want a mentor. Write down all the reasons you need a mentor and be able to articulate them. Think about what you would like to gain from the relationship as well.

Know your preferred work style. Think about your personality type and that of your mentors. Some mentors are very laid back and friendly, others can be very structured and formal. It's just a difference in personality work styles.

Mentors are not perfect. They are regular people willing to be a resource to help you learn. Your mentor can advise you, but making decisions should always be your responsibility.

Describe who your ideal mentor would be. Take into consideration the person's experience, qualifications and current position. Make a list of those qualities.

Make a list of people who might fit your criteria. We all would like a high-profile person as a mentor, but sometimes the best mentors are not high-profile people. Don't get star-struck. Start with a dedicated, lesser known person who is genuinely interested in your improvement.

Tell a few trusted people you are searching for a mentor. If you see someone you think might fit your description of the ideal person, invite him or her to coffee or schedule an informational interview. During your meeting, ask that person if it's acceptable for you to call occasionally for advice. Most people will say yes, but if the person sounds hesitant, he could be uninterested or have too many other time commitments. Don't take it personally. Thank the person for his time and move on to the next person on your list. If the person says yes, great.

Look at your school, company and community. Find out if your company/school has a formal mentoring program. If so, check to see if there are any prerequisites.

Don't be a leech. Although your mentor is supposed to help you, don't suck him dry of his time, talents, and resources. Figure out what you can also offer your mentor so it becomes a mutually beneficial relationship. Be prepared, enthusiastic and show you understand and appreciate their time and information.

THE VALUE OF VOLUNTEERING

A quick easy way to build your résumé is through volunteering. It does not matter that you are not getting paid; what matters is that you are learning new skills, strengthening the ones you already possess, and building a network of friends and mentors who can help each other. Even if you have a strong résumé with work experience, companies want to see that you are a well-rounded individual and that you care about other things besides making money. Always make sure that you are actively engaged in a volunteer opportunity throughout your career.

Find an organization that you feel passionate about. Do you light up when helping the homeless? Consider volunteering at a soup kitchen, collecting food or taking part in a clothing drive.

Make a commitment and show up. Many nonprofit organizations rely heavily on volunteers to run their programs. When you commit to a schedule, treat it with the same respect you would give a paid position and show up regularly.

Call ahead. If you will be late or will need to miss a day, give your volunteer coordinator ample time to find a replacement.

Meet new people. This is the time to meet people in a non-threatening environment. Take the time to get to know your fellow volunteers and feel free to share your dreams and aspirations.

Stay in touch. Remain in contact in a healthy professional manner with other volunteers as this builds your network.

Do a little extra. Don't just do what you are asked to do; look for ways you can give even more.

As always, bring a great attitude. Volunteers are supposed to be a positive addition to organizations that need help. Make sure you are pleasant and easy to work with.

Respect the rules. Depending on where you volunteer, there may be duties you cannot perform. Follow all the safety procedures and guidelines. They are for your protection and that of the organization.

Be humble. You are not better than anyone else because you volunteer. You will probably soon learn that you benefit more when you share your time and expertise with others.

CHAPTER EIGHT

PEOPLE SKILLS

- Working with Your Supervisor

- Interacting with Co-Workers

- Valuing Diversity

- Body Talk

- Listening 101

- Problem-Solving Skills

- Language Skills

Did you know?

Clans of long ago that wanted to get rid of their unwanted people without killing them used to burn their houses down - hence the expression "to get fired."

WORKING WITH YOUR SUPERVISOR

Supervisors are in charge because the company has confidence in their ability to perform supervisory responsibilities and obtain the results the company needs to make a profit. A supervisor's role is to guide employees to become the best worker each can be by developing their skills. This is not always easy, but every employee needs to know how to work with his or her supervisor and build a professional relationship. You do not have to be best friends with your supervisor, but you must relate to your supervisor with respectful courtesy. You can learn a lot!

1. Be willing to learn.
Show your supervisor that you are eager to learn, try new things, and do extra tasks.

2. Be proactive.
Whenever there is a problem, immediately notify your supervisor if you are not able to resolve the issue. Don't waste time on it.

3. Speak up.
Some jobs that young people do are quite boring but are absolutely essential to the company. Ask your supervisor to vary the tasks that you do and try to identify areas you would like to learn more about.

4. Understand the company.
Learn how your daily responsibilities help the company. Seeing how your contributions assist the company will make you a better employee when you recognize how important your role is.

5. Ask for clarification.

Always ask questions when in doubt. Do not feel intimidated or shy. It's better to ask many questions and do a task well than to guess what is wanted and make errors.

6. Follow directions.

It sounds simple, but it can be difficult. Employee and supervisor relationships are more productive when an employee can follow instructions from the supervisor.

7. Be innovative.

Look for ways to improve the processes in your area and share those with your supervisor, but don't make changes without first getting approval to go ahead.

INTERACTING WITH CO-WORKERS

Chances are you will not be working by yourself all the time. Therefore, it is critical that you develop your people skills and foster professional relationships with co-workers based on respect.

Respect is earned as relationships develop and people get to know each other. Always show respect to others even when they may be disrespectful to you. This will demonstrate your maturity and your respect for yourself. Here are some ways to build goodwill with co-workers:

Keep personal business private.
It's difficult not to show feelings and emotions. However, in a workplace setting, whether it's retail, a supermarket, a shop or an office, try not to make your personal life a topic of discussion.

Keep it clean.
Not many people like to clean after up after others. If you've been assigned a workstation, keep it clean and organized.

Respect your co-worker's space.
In the event you need to use a co-worker's workspace, keep it clean and neat and do not rummage through the desk or locker.

Smile please.
Even when it's been a hard day and life seems impossible, try to smile and be a welcoming face to those around you.

"Please" and "thank you."
These little words are critical. People judge you positively or negatively when you use them and when you don't. Use them often.

Listen to your tone of voice.
The tone of voice you use when speaking with others is
determined by how you feel at that moment when
addressing someone. Anger, frustration or sarcasm are
easily detected. Be aware of this while speaking.

Think before you joke around.
Jokes that are harsh, discriminating or in questionable taste
should not be told. They are offensive and can cause
discord in the workplace. If co-workers are telling these
jokes, walk away and do not encourage or laugh with
them.

Know your limit.
It's easy to be influenced by adults or friends on the job.
Learn from responsible workers and never imitate co-
workers who break company policies, no matter how
small.

Own your mistakes.
All humans make mistakes. Honest mature people own
their mistakes and bear the consequences.

Limit socializing.
Casually visiting co-workers at their work areas should
not become a habit. It is a distraction and interrupts the
workflow.

VALUING DIVERSITY

It is important for all employees to be able to work with all people regardless of their ethnicity, religion, race, personality, limited ability or personal life.

If you are still in school, it's easy to avoid the people you do not like, but at some point in your career you will be asked to work with someone you do not like or agree with. The important thing to remember is that you are at work to get the job done; you are not required to like this person, but you must treat everybody with respect and courtesy.

1. It's not the outward appearance that counts; it's the quality of work.

2. Priority number one is always to get the job done well and on time.

3. Professionalism is not about liking someone; it's learning to respect everyone.

4. Get to know someone you don't like and find out why they act and think the way they do; you may be surprised.

5. Right now someone somewhere does not like you because of how you look, talk, dress, or work. How would you want them to treat you?

6. Learn to value your co-workers based on the quality of their work, not on your personal feelings towards them.

7. Don't judge people based on popular stereotypes. Think for yourself and make your own conclusions.

Regardless of what you do in life, chances are you will probably be working side by side with people from different countries, cultures, language, religion, personality and lifestyle. It's actually a great thing for companies to have a diverse staff as they will produce better solutions for their customers. There is strength in differences. Problems arise when we try to make people all the same.

BODY TALK

Yes, your body talks and people pay more attention to your body language than the actual words you say. There is an old saying, "Your actions speak so loud I can't hear what you are saying." Let your words and body say the same thing!

Be mindful of what your body is communicating to those around you as there are both positive and negative body languages.

Negative Body Language

The following are perceived as negative body signals that communicate nervousness, insecurity, frustration, anger, or defensiveness: *head shaking, eyes rolling up with a shrug, crossed arms, sideways glances, checking the time, frowning, fidgeting, biting fingernails, chewing pens or pencils, hissing, pointing a finger, and tapping or twitching a foot.*

Positive Body Language

The following signals are positive body language that present you as a person of confidence, cooperation, and openness: *standing tall, sitting up straight, holding chin up, smiling, holding steepled, upturned or open hands, holding your hands behind your back when standing, leaning forward and tilting head toward speaker.*

6 Steps to a Powerful Handshake

- Offer your right hand
- Web of the hand to web of the other person's hand
- Give eye contact
- Firm grip (if it's a man shaking a woman's hand)
- Two pumps
- Smile

In many western countries, these give the impression that you are confident.

<u>Note:</u> *In some countries, maintaining eye contact can actually be a sign of disrespect. Make sure to adhere to the customs of the country where you are working.*

LISTENING 101

There is a technique to listening. Normally when people speak, it is so easy not to listen to the other person. We are preoccupied trying to figure out how to respond and get our point across.

Having good listening skills will help you interact better with others as you learn to listen to spoken words and also what is not said. If you want to make a good impression, just close your mouth and open your ears. You'll be amazed at what you will learn. Practice your listening skills often. Good listeners do the following:

- **Maintain eye contact.**
Do not stare, but do look at the person to whom you are speaking, glance away once in a while, then look back. This indicates your interest and respect for that person.

- **Show interest.**
Nod your head, say words like "uh-huh," "I see," "really" and "okay." These all indicate to the speaker that you're listening.

- **Do not interrupt.**
Allow the speaker time to finish his/her thoughts before you begin to speak.

- **Paraphrase what you understand.**
Repeat back to the speaker what you heard. Start off by saying something like, "Did I hear you correctly..." and repeat what you understood and then allow the speaker to correct you if you misunderstood some information. Even if you didn't get it exactly right, the speaker will feel good that you tried to really understand.

PROBLEM-SOLVING SKILLS

Resolving problems quickly and in a sensible way is essential at school and also in the workplace. Small concerns can balloon into big issues when the right problem-solving techniques are not applied.

Here are a few ways to look at problems and come up with solutions quickly and safely.

1. When someone offends you, try not to lose your temper. Walk away, calm down, and think about how you would like to approach the person. It must be a calm conversation.

2. Talk over the problem with a neutral adult to brainstorm ways to resolve the issue.

3. Never try to resolve a problem when you are angry, frustrated, or tired. Take a break, get rested, then come back to it. Don't try to ignore it or forget as it could happen again if it is not resolved the first time.

4. Think about the results you want. It is difficult to vow never to speak to a co-worker again. Be sensible and make sound decisions.

5. Violence, cursing, verbal abuse, or getting even are never options.

LANGUAGE SKILLS

Young people have a language all to themselves, but proper English is expected in the workplace. Slang or broken English is inappropriate for the workplace, even though it may be okay in other settings.

- Profanity is an absolute no-no!

- Derogatory words, demeaning gestures, and racial or religious slurs are never acceptable at work.

- Listen to how others around you speak, preferably those in authority. Most times they provide a good example to follow.

- Talk to an English teacher and practice speaking proper English regardless of whether English is your first or second language.

- Filler words such as *umm, you know, like* and *you know what I mean* reflect poorly on your ability to articulate thoughts and ideas.

CHAPTER NINE

CUSTOMER SERVICE

- Making Customers Happy

- When Customers Make You Mad

Did you know?

A good customer experience is told to 8 other people. A bad customer experience is told to 22 other people.

MAKING CUSTOMERS HAPPY

"Our customers are number one." "The customer is always right." These are slogans that many companies have adopted. What does that mean for you as a worker?

Many young people have jobs dealing directly with customers and pleasing the customer is crucial for any business to stay open. The way a customer is treated will determine if he/she will come back again. Repeat clients make a company profitable and every customer is important. Take the time to go the extra mile as often as you can.

What makes a customer happy?

Call them by name.
If you know the customer's name, use it. It makes them feel special. If you do not know their name, address the customer as "Sir" or "Ma'am."

Acknowledge customers immediately.
Greet customers as soon as they enter by saying "hello," "welcome," "good morning," "good evening," or "be right with you." If unable to verbally communicate at the moment, use body language, smiles, or hand signals to acknowledge them.

Listen to customers.
Almost everyone craves undivided attention. Listen with your body, or give verbal affirmations if on the phone (see section on "Listening 101").

Be flexible.
Know your company's policies. Some customers may require a bit more to please them; it's called going the extra mile.

Say "Thank you and have a nice day!"
Again, make each customer feel special. Let them see that you do appreciate them.

Understand the customer profile.
Customers have habits and needs that make them shop in different places. When you understand them, it's easier to make them feel like number one. You will then be able to anticipate and meet their needs before they even ask.

WHEN CUSTOMERS MAKE YOU MAD

Is the customer really always right? No, the customer is not really always right, but the company wants customers to feel special. Not every customer is wonderful to serve. Some people are just hard to please; they complain and seem to be always in a bad mood.

Sometimes the company is to blame because the policies do not meet the needs of the customer. Sometimes another employee has been rude to the customer. The mark of a true professional, adult or teenager, is how that difficult customer is treated. What techniques can you use to please this type of customer?

- **Stay calm.**
They may not be angry with you. More than likely it's the company and its policies, not you personally. Be aware of your attitude and remain positive.

- **Be patient.**
Listen to their complaints with your body, voice, and imagination to hear their real needs.

- **Apologize quickly.**
Customers just want companies to take responsibility. Saying "I'm sorry" helps the customers feel better. Be genuine in your apology, even if you are not personally to blame. You are speaking for the company.

- **Help them.**
Fix their problem if you can. That's all most upset customers want.

- **Never argue with customers.**

Even when you know they are wrong, never argue with customers. It proves nothing, no one really wins, and your supervisor could bring disciplinary actions against you.

- **Refer to your supervisor.**

When you are unable to assist a customer, ask someone with more authority or knowledge such as a supervisor or co-worker to help resolve the issue.

CHAPTER TEN

ON-THE-JOB PERFORMANCE

- Understanding Performance Appraisals

- Supervisor's Feedback

- My Professional Skill Sets

Did you know?

It takes 72 muscles to frown, but only 13 to smile.

UNDERSTANDING PERFORMANCE APPRAISALS

A performance appraisal, performance evaluation or performance review is the equivalent of getting a report card for the work you perform on the job. Some companies do it on a quarterly or annual basis or every two weeks for summer employees, and some organizations do not do it at all.

The appraisal looks at three main areas:

1. It measures your performance.
Supervisors use appraisals to determine who gets promoted and who receives bonuses and salary increases. It is your responsibility as much as it is your supervisor's to know how you are performing. Prepare for your appraisal by keeping track of all the projects you complete and any feedback you receive along the way. The information in your appraisal should not be a surprise if you are having regular conversations with your supervisor.

2. It identifies areas of development.
Your appraisal should reveal your areas of strengths and the areas that need improving. If the company is pleased with your performance and resources are available, then they mostly likely will invest in you by providing training and development opportunities to enhance your skills. It's also a great goal-setting tool that allows you to grow professionally.

3. It helps the company make decisions.
Companies merge, downsize, reorganize and expand on a regular basis, and in many cases the performance evaluations are key to helping the company decide who

should stay when downsizing and who should be promoted when expanding.

Some companies do a great job of evaluating their employees and others do not. That's why it is your job to communicate with your supervisor on a regular basis to see how you are doing.

EXERCISE

Use this space to begin the process of a self-evaluation.

My Job Title:_____

My Daily Tasks:

1.

2.

3.

4.

5.

What skills are you developing? (Refer back to the page in Chapter 1 that lists the skills employers need in their employees.)

Skills:

1.

2.

3.

4.

5.

SUPERVISOR'S FEEDBACK

It is your supervisor's responsibility to guide you on the job. It is your responsibility to listen and strive to constantly improve the quality of your work and interaction with customers and co-workers. Ultimately, you are the one who will either benefit from having great work habits or lose out because you have not learned how to observe, listen, and learn from your supervisor and your general work environment.

Talk with your supervisor and let that person know you would like to get feedback on how you are doing as a worker. Then record this information so you can track your progress. Remember, you do not have to like your supervisor; just respect him.

The following pages are reserved for your supervisor to give his/her feedback on your performance.

PERFORMANCE APPRAISAL

To be completed by supervisor:

Please take a few moments to rate the performance of this employee.

Employee:_____

Position: _____ _____

Good job! You are doing well in the following areas.

Let's work on improving these areas.

Personality: I'm impressed by your ability to...

Goal Setting:

This is what I would like to see you accomplish in...

1 month

3 months

6 months

Comments:

_____   _____
Supervisor   Employee

MY PROFESSIONAL SKILL SETS

Now that you have had a chance to evaluate your job and have been evaluated by your supervisor, take a few moments to list your skills.

I am confident that I am proficient at the following skills:

1.

2.

3.

4.

5.

CHAPTER ELEVEN

JUSTICE ON THE JOB

- Your Legal Rights

- Sexual Harassment

- Drug Testing in the Workplace

Did you know?

Thirty-five percent of high school students reported that they experienced sexual harassment in their part-time work.

YOUR LEGAL RIGHTS

This section is applicable to workers in the United States only. Each country has its own labor laws. Please refer to your country's laws.

You need to know that there are government rules that are designed to protect you on the job. These rules cover the number of hours you are allowed to work, what kinds of jobs you may have, and your employer's obligation to provide a safe environment in which to work. Here are general answers to commonly asked questions. Each state can set its own rules so it is always wise to check for specific information for your state.

Q. How old do I have to be to get a job?
A. In most states, 14 and 15 year olds are allowed to work but on a limited basis.

Q. Are there any jobs for youths under 14?
A. Yes, you can work as a newspaper carrier, entertainer, perform domestic work (babysitting, party help, yard care), a golf course caddie, or if you are at least 12 years old you can work on a farm.

Q. Do I have to have a work permit if I'm 14 or 15?
A. Many states require 14 and 15 year olds to obtain "working papers," also called a "work permit," before they begin working. Check with your school counselors or Department of Labor as some states also require a signed letter from your doctor before you can begin working.

Q. How many hours can I work if I'm 14 or 15?
A. During the school year:
> 3 hours per day, 18 hours a week,
> 7 a.m. - 7 p.m., not during school hours

On weekends:
> 8 hours per day on weekends and holidays

During the summer:
> 8 hours per day, 40 hours per week

Q. Can my school stop me from working if I do not keep my grades up?
A. Yes. If you are working because you received a working permit or working papers, the counselor who issued the permit can revoke your right to work until your grades improve.

Q. I'm 16. What hours can I work?
A. Some states have restrictions on the number of hours 16 and 17 year olds can work. Check with your school about your individual state.

Q. Are there jobs I cannot get?
A. If you are under 18 years old, you cannot work in jobs considered to be dangerous such as manufacturing, driving vehicles, storing of explosives, logging, roofing, excavation, wrecking, demolition, slaughtering, meat packing and meat processing.

Also, you are not allowed to operate, clean, set up, adjust, or repair any of the following: food slicers, grinders, choppers, cutters, and commercial mixers. Power machinery such as saws (all types), hoisting equipment, guillotine shears, and metal-forming machinery fall under this category as well.

Q. What should I do if my supervisor asks me to perform a dangerous or hazardous task?
A. Calmly remind your supervisor that because of your age you are not allowed to perform such duties. If the incident occurs again, report it to the Human Resources office, a parent, school counselor or trusted adult.

Q. Do these rules apply when I am in a vocational education program?
A. Students in vocational education programs who are expected to work with machinery or under conditions deemed hazardous or dangerous need to check with school officials for specific guidelines that govern apprenticeships.

Q. How much am I supposed to be paid?
A. Federal law states that your starting wage must be at least the current minimum wage.

Q. How much is overtime pay?
A. People who work over 40 hours are eligible for overtime. Overtime, or time-and-a-half, means you will be paid 1.5 times your hourly wage. If your regular hourly wage is $7 per hour, then you will receive $10.50 per hour for each overtime hour worked.

SEXUAL HARASSMENT

One area of workplace behavior that young people must understand in order to be successful is sexual harassment. Some school environments, even though sexual harassment policies are in place, tend not to be as strict as workplaces. Young people often do not address sexual harassment as they do not want to stand out in the crowd or be labeled a snitch or tattletale.

Q. What is sexual harassment?
A. It is unwelcome sexual advances, requests for sexual favors, verbal statements or physical contacts that are of a sexual nature, or displaying objects or pictures that are sexually suggestive.

Q. Can males be sexually harassed?
A. Yes. Sexual harassment affects men and women, boys and girls.

Q. Is sexual harassment only between persons of the opposite sex?
A. No. Sexual harassment can also occur female to female or male to male.

Q. What should I do if I think I've been sexually harassed?
A. Report the incident to a supervisor immediately, and also be sure to ask a parent, teacher, or trusted adult to support you.

Q. What should I do if my supervisor is the offender?
A. Report the incident to the Human Resources office immediately, and also be sure to ask a parent, teacher, or trusted adult to support you.

Q. When should I report incidents of sexual harassment?
A. Immediately. Do not wait, and also be sure to ask a parent, teacher, or trusted adult to support you.

Q. Is flirting sexual harassment?
A. It can only be classified as sexual harassment if the person you have an interest in considers this behavior unwanted and unwelcome.

Q. Is dressing in a suggestive manner inviting sexual harassment?
A. Let's be realistic. The way you dress may cause some heads to turn, but it's not an invitation to be sexually harassed. At the same time, use good judgment and avoid dressing in clothes that are clearly questionable.

Q. How do I know if the person does not like my behavior?
A. You can always ask. The person can let you know verbally or with her or his body language. When you are told "no," you must accept it, even if you don't believe it.

Q. Can I be fired if I tell?
A. No. The law is designed to protect your job. If you are the victim, you should not be penalized for exercising your right to protect yourself.

DRUG TESTING IN THE WORKPLACE

Some employers may require that you take a drug test when applying for work. This is legal as companies need to protect themselves to ensure all employees are coherent enough to perform their jobs without putting themselves, the company, or other employees at risk.

Q. What kind of test is utilized?
A. There are generally two types: the urine test and the hair sample. The urine test is more common. You may be asked to give a urine sample and that is usually tested for marijuana, cocaine and other illegal substances, or you could be asked for a hair sample and that can be tested for marijuana as well as other drugs.

Q. What do I need to bring to the test?
A. If you are under 18 years old, you must provide a parental consent form before being tested. Everyone is required to provide a picture ID.

You will need to fill out a medical questionnaire. Be sure to answer ALL questions; do not leave any questions unanswered. Ask an adult for help if you are unsure how to answer a question.

Q. What if I'm on medication?
A. If you are on any kind of medication or you've taken any kind of over-the-counter medicine, including all painkillers, you should indicate that on the medical questionnaire you fill out before taking the test.

Q. If I am around people who smoke marijuana, can I test positive even though I was not smoking?
A. There is a possibility that you may test positive depending on your metabolism. If you inhale smoke from marijuana cigarettes, you may test positive.

Q. What happens if I fail the drug test?
A. You will be denied employment. You will fail a drug test if your sample is positive for any illegal substances.

Q. How long do drugs stay in your system?
A. That depends on your body type, your weight, height, and body metabolism. Don't depend on taking substances that promise to clean all traces of drugs from your system if you really want a job. Your best bet is not to take drugs at all.

CHAPTER TWELVE

MONEY MATTERS

- Understanding Your Paycheck

- Managing a Checking Account

- Using a Credit Card

- Saving and Investing Your Money

- Are You Living Above Your Means?

- Need vs. Want

- Building a Budget

Did you know?

All 50 states are listed across the top of the Lincoln Memorial on the back of the $5 bill.

UNDERSTANDING YOUR PAYCHECK

It's wonderful to see the face of a person when they get their first paycheck. It goes from excited to utter disbelief and confusion. This expression comes as they try to figure out the deductions and calculate the amount of hours worked and how much they are supposed to receive. To help ease some of that confusion, here are a few tips.

Q. Who withholds money from my check and why?
A. The employer does for the government. Money can be taken out for Social Security and Medicare taxes known as the Federal Insurance Contributions Act (FICA) and for state and federal income taxes. ***Note: This applies to the United States only.***

Q. How do I know what I am being paid?
A. Before you start working, ask what your hourly rate will be and whether you're eligible for overtime. Multiply the number of hours worked times your hourly rate (calculate overtime hours separately), and that is the amount due you before withholding.

Q. How often do I get paid?
A. That depends on the company you work for. Some companies pay biweekly and some pay weekly. Ask your supervisor what schedule your company uses.

Q. What should I do if there is an error in my check?
A. Approach your supervisor in a CALM manner, state your case and ask him/her to help you figure out the error. To avoid problems, copy your time sheet every week and keep accurate records. If you punch a clock, have a book and keep track of all your hours so you will have a backup record to help support your case if an error occurs.

Q. Do I have to file taxes?
A. Students are usually exempt from filing taxes because they do not make a significant amount of money. However, some students earn over the limit and will need to file. Talk with the person who prepares your family's taxes or a school career counselor.

MANAGING A CHECKING ACCOUNT

As soon as you get your first check, choose a local bank and open both savings and checking accounts. You need a checking account as it is not wise to carry large sums of cash. There are different types of checking accounts. Shop around the different banks, and credit unions if you are eligible, and see which one has the type of account that is best for you. Here are a few hints:

No minimum balance. Find an account that does not require a minimum balance. This is important as some banks and credit unions charge a fee if you do not maintain a certain balance.

Overdraft protection. Get an account with an overdraft protection package as part of your checking account. In the event you have insufficient funds in your checking account, the bank will automatically go to your overdraft protection account (usually a savings account) to deduct funds to cover the transaction.

Get a debit card. A debit card is like a credit card, but you can only charge up to the amount of money in your account. It's very convenient and it comes with a credit card logo so no one knows the difference.

Ask about fees. There are fees to check balances by phone or computer, ATM fees at your bank or if you use another bank's ATM machine, fees for insufficient funds if you are overdrawn, fees for bounced checks you receive, fees for paying bills online, and the list can go on.

Transaction limitations. Some banks have limitations on the number of transactions you can make before being charged a fee, such as the number of checks allowed monthly or the number of debit card transactions. Know what they are and manage wisely.

Balancing your checkbook. If you know how to balance a checkbook, keeping your finances in order as an adult will be much easier. Get a head start.

1. Record the opening balance for the account. This is the amount of money in your initial deposit. Remember to enter the fee for ordering checks.

2. Record all checks. Before you tear a check from the checkbook, always record the transaction in the check register, the amount of the check, to whom the check is written, the number of the check, the date the check is written, and then calculate the new balance.

3. Record all deposits. As soon as you make a deposit, record it in the addition column of the checkbook and then calculate the new balance. Keep the deposit slip in your records.

4. Subtract fees. If your bank charges fees for ATM transactions or other types of fees, be sure to subtract those as well.

5. Add the interest rate. The interest rates for checking accounts are usually very low, but you still need to add the interest rate to balance your account. The easiest way to do this is when you get your monthly statement.

6. Balance your monthly statement. At the end of each month, it's important to check your statement for accuracy. Check off the checks that have been cashed, and remember that sometimes even though you have written a check, it takes a few days to register in your account. Make sure you have the same balance as the bank for the items on the statement.

7. Troubleshooting your account. In the event your checkbook does not balance, double check all transactions and ensure you deducted all fees, checks, and ATM transactions and added interest rates. The bank will charge a fee to help you so use that only as a last resort, but that is still cheaper than ruining your credit record by being overdrawn.

USING A CREDIT CARD

There are advertisements everywhere sending messages that once you have a credit card, you will have no worries, the sky is the limit, and you can have a great time with family and friends. Having a credit card is not a right; it is a privilege that should be handled responsibly for there are serious long-term consequences when credit cards are mismanaged. When you obtain a credit card, you are agreeing with the credit card company to pay back in full all the debt you owe.

Getting a Credit Card

Young adults who are 18 years or older can obtain a credit card in their own name. Teens under 18 can obtain a supplemental card from parents or other family member. You will be issued a card, but the bill will be included in the primary cardholder's monthly statement.

Parents or guardians can co-sign a credit card application. This means that in the event you are unable to make the payments, the co-signer (your parent or guardian) will be held responsible for all unpaid debts.

Finally, you can open a savings or checking account at a local bank and apply for a credit card from the bank. You can be granted a card if you agree to keep a certain amount of money in the account with the understanding that if you do not make your monthly payments the bank will automatically deduct the money from your savings or checking account.

Managing a Credit Card

1. Fees

• *Credit cards are not free.* Companies charge you to use their cards. There are lots of fees attached to credit cards, and they differ according to the type of credit card. Responsible credit card users are aware of all the fees for all aspects of the account.

• *Annual fees:* The amount of money the credit card company charges you just to have a card, varies $0-$75 (some cards do not charge an annual fee).

• *Transaction fees:* The amount charged if you take out a cash advance is usually higher than your regular interest rate and accrues daily.

• *Interest rate:* This, too, varies with cards. Some have low introductory rates for a limited time, then the rate increases significantly after the introductory period ends.

• *Late fees:* All credit cards charge late fees for payments received after the due date, and your interest rate will be increased when you pay late.

2. Pay more than the minimum.
The monthly bill states the minimum payment due. Always pay more than the minimum. This will decrease the amount of interest you pay on your balance. Credit card companies make money when you pay only the minimum.

3. Check your monthly statement.
Verify your statement each month to make sure you made all the charges that are listed.

4. Keep all receipts. Your receipts from purchases will serve as a second record for your transactions in the event there is an error on your monthly statement.

5. Secure cards. Always keep your card in a safe location and do not lend to anyone, friends or family!

6. Lost or misplaced cards. Report lost or misplaced cards immediately, preferably within 24 hours. Make a copy of the front and back of all your credit cards along with the number to call to report lost or stolen cards and keep in a separate location from your cards.

7. Credit Bureaus. Credit bureaus keep a record of your credit history. It's basically a report card of your credit worthiness: do you pay bills on time, how much you owe, how many times did you pay your bills late, the names of the companies you owe, etc.

Long-Term Effects

If you are not responsible with your credit now, it will affect your ability to finance a car loan or home mortgage, get loans to pay for school, and even a career, especially if you are interested in a career in finance.

SAVING AND INVESTING YOUR MONEY

It's an exciting and powerful feeling when you make your own money, but it can be devastating if proper money management skills are not used.

What you do with your money depends on your reason for working. Some young people need to work to help the family, provide for their baby, buy a car, or save for college. Whatever your reason, it is critical that you budget to save a percentage of your income.

Q. Why do I need a budget?
A. Having a budget will help you understand what you can afford. Try not to invest your paycheck in expensive designer brand-name clothing, sneakers or even partying. Snacks and fast food can also decrease your savings significantly.

Q. Why bother to save?
A. Building wealth begins when you save more than you spend. To afford the things you want now and later, it's imperative to set aside funds that will earn interest and make money for you.

Q. How much should I save?
A. Whenever possible, try to set aside at least 50% of your earnings. If that is not possible due to family obligations, aim to save between 10-25% each pay period.

Q. Can I invest in the stock market?
A. Yes, you can. Of course, before investing have an in-depth conversation with a trusted adult who can help you figure out your goals and choose a financial advisor to set up your accounts.

Q. Where can I invest my money?

A. There are lots of financial services companies that can help you invest. Again, ask your parents, teachers, or other adults to refer you to a creditable investment agency. Take an adult with you and ask lots of questions.

Q. What options do I have if I do not want to invest in the stock market?

A. Open a regular savings account or a CD (Certificate of Deposit) at your local bank or credit union.

ARE YOU LIVING ABOVE YOUR MEANS?

If you have money to buy what you want, does that necessarily mean you can afford the purchase? The following are some conditions that indicate you are buying more than you can afford:

1. Putting items on credits cards and only making the minimum payments.

2. Borrowing money from friends.

3. Neglecting important responsibilities (health care, paying utility bills, etc.) to get what you want.

4. Buying what you want, when you want, and you have no savings account.

5. Having a savings account but rarely funding it, or you are constantly withdrawing from your savings.

Can you afford it?
Imagine there is a leather jacket that you want (not need). If, after you have taken care of all your expenses and obligations, there is money left over (disposable income) then you can afford to buy the jacket.

Friendly reminder: Think twice before you spend your money, and live within your means.

NEED vs. WANT

There is a big difference between a need and a want. Unfortunately, many people have difficulty distinguishing between needs and wants.

Need. A need is something you cannot live without. It's an absolute necessity, a requirement for living. Food, sleep, water, clothing, heat and medical attention are some of the basic needs of life.

Want. A want is something you desire. It would be nice if you had it. These things might make life more comfortable, more fun, make you look fabulous, but they are not necessities. Designer clothing, specialty foods and cable television are all examples of wants. What has happened is many people classify their wants as needs. Some young people do not want to live without these luxuries, or perhaps other people paid for these previously and they are used to having them without having to pay for them.

Examine the things you currently have in your life that you classify as needs and wants and list them below.

My Needs   **My Wants**

BUILDING A BUDGET

Take a few minutes to look at how you spend your money.

Savings and Investments   _____
> (Tip: Save at least 10% per paycheck. 10% of your paycheck is calculated in this way: Paycheck (net income after taxes) is $800 and 10% of $800 is $80. Put $80 in your savings account right away before you pay any expenses.)

Food (snacks)	_____
Car payments	_____
Car insurance	_____
Clothing	_____
Entertainment	_____
Cable	_____
Home phone	_____
Cell phone	_____
Monthly internet service	_____
Other	_____
Other	_____

Total Monthly Expenditures   _____

Total Monthly Income   _____

Difference   _____

EXERCISE

Look at your budget again. Are there things you have classified as needs that really are wants?

Can you eliminate any of the expenses in your budget to allow more money to go towards your savings?

Does your budget take into consideration your needs:

1. To save for college, a place to live if applicable.

2. Living expenses (rent, utilities, food) if you plan to work full time after high school.

3. Your need/desire to help your family with living expenses.

CHAPTER THIRTEEN

EXPLORING THE INTERNATIONAL WORKPLACE

- Americans Traveling Overseas for Internships

- Coming to the United States for an Internship

AMERICANS TRAVELING OVERSEAS FOR INTERNSHIPS

If you have the opportunity to travel abroad and work, take advantage of it. Working internationally is an asset that can open doors in many companies if you have aspirations to be in senior level positions. Even if you are in high school, it's not too early to get some international experience. International travel can change your life. It's an opportunity to see a world you have probably read about or seen on television. An internship can help you to experience it firsthand professionally and socially. Making the transition can be tricky so let's show you how to make the move go smoothly.

Get to know the country. There are lots of travel guides and internet sites to give you a bird's eye view of your new country. Don't just visit the party sites; do research on different aspects of the country.

Don't be an "Ugly American." Many times it seems you can spot an American a mile away, loud and improperly dressed. Be gracious and follow the dress code of the country, especially if you are in a Muslim country where women must cover their heads.

Learn the language. It is to your advantage to learn the local language even if you will be speaking English at work. Understand the basics of asking for directions, ordering in a restaurant, saying "no thank you "graciously and expressing gratitude.

Try new foods. Do not immediately seek out the closest McDonald's, Subway or Kentucky Fried Chicken. Take the time to explore the local cuisine, and please do not make negative comments or faces with foods you may not find appealing to your taste buds.

142

Stay away from drugs. No matter how inviting and easy it may seem in a foreign country, resist the urge to experiment with drugs while traveling. Many Americans have been imprisoned for drug possession overseas, and being locked up overseas is no picnic.

Limit alcohol. Many countries do not enforce a strict drinking age and to Americans who are not accustomed to such responsibility it can be dangerous. Some families make it a custom to have a small glass of wine with dinner. If you do, think about your after-dinner activities and location before saying yes. Think before you drink.

Learn the customs. In some countries, men and women have very distinct roles. Study the country you are visiting to see if this applies and respect those roles.

Minimize the need to be a savior. There are countries that need external help but don't feel you need to fix everything that seems wrong in your eyes. Be respectful of the cultural practices and developmental stage of a country. If you see an area where improvement is needed, approaching the right person in the right way will be beneficial to all.

Recognize the time tradition. In America everything is time driven and it is impolite to keep someone waiting. In other countries, however, it is more than acceptable to keep someone waiting. In fact, many appointments can start an hour or two after the appointed time and that is the norm. Don't get upset; just relax and make sure you are prepared. Use the extra time wisely!

Build the relationship, and then the business comes.
Time is often spent socializing first before any business is
conducted. Don't try to change people and rush them
through the process, just go with the flow. In some
countries, time is not money, relationships are.

Meet the locals and find new peer groups. Try to connect
with a local family who can give you an authentic
experience minus the tourist attractions and spending
traps. These are relationships that can last into your
adulthood. Treasure them if you are able to make that
possible. Don't just socialize with the other Americans.
Spend most of your time becoming familiar with the
language, culture and customs.

Observe safety precautions. Don't develop a false sense
of security, especially when visiting smaller nations. Ask
your host/company what you need to know in order to
stay safe.

Is it love or lust? You've probably watched the movies
with story lines of finding love in another country. Don't
be deceived. The people you meet in another country are
just like the ones you left at home with issues that only
look different. Don't jeopardize your career or your life for
a short fling.

COMING TO THE UNITED STATES
FOR AN INTERNSHIP

If you are growing up outside the United States and you have the opportunity to work or intern at a company in the United States, you are in for quite a treat and some big cultural differences. Having grown up on the Caribbean island of St. Vincent and the Grenadines and migrating to the United States as a teenager myself, the transition took a little time. Pay attention to the information shared in this book to help position you to do well socially and professionally.

Each of the states that make up the United States are similar in many ways, yet very different. Regardless of where you spend your time, take the opportunity to get to know the people and customs.

You need to be outspoken. Although in some countries being outspoken is viewed as inappropriate, this is not so in the United States. People expect you to speak up for yourself, and in some states they do so in a manner that you may perceive as rude. Watch and observe before you pass judgment.

Be careful with stereotypes. Much of what you may know about the United States and its people was probably framed by the media. Do not buy into the racial stereotypes that may be depicted in the media about different groups.

Practice your English. If English is your second, third or even fourth language, practice as much as possible. It's an ugly truth but some people are not as patient with heavy accents. Don't get discouraged; the only way to get clearer is to practice.

Listen for slang. If you meet friends who speak slang, know that this is not the norm in the work world. Slang is the casual use of words, and some words can actually mean the opposite of their real meaning; e.g., " bad" in some circles can actually mean "good" depending on how it is used.

Understanding accents. Different regions of the United States may pronounce the same word differently so ask questions if you are not sure.

Get involved. The fastest and best way to immerse yourself in a culture is to volunteer. Whether at work or in the community where you live, offer your time to help others.

Limit time with your homeland friends. Like any person, international students and workers find comfort in the familiar. Resist the urge to spend most of your time with people from your country, especially if your native tongue is not English. This slows your understanding of the American culture, people and language.

Pace yourself. New York is known as the city that never sleeps; there is always something to do and places to go. Pace yourself and don't try to do everything all at once. Manage your time and health so you can last throughout your internship and leave with a positive experience regardless of where you may reside while in the United States.

Be street smart. America like any other country has elements of life that are not so attractive. Although there are lots of people who mean well, there are just as many who are looking for the easy way out. Ask your host/ organization about safety precautions for your area.

Focus on your American dream. This truly is the place where dreams are made, but you have to pay your dues. If anyone promises you a quick easy way to make your dreams come true, it's probably a scam. Work hard, stay focused, ask for what you want, build quality relationships and chances are you will succeed, but not overnight.

Watch out for the love bug. Foreign accents can be a love magnet for many people who may find you attractive. Protect yourself as it's easy to get carried away and find yourself in life-threatening situations.

Find a mentor. This is an invaluable tool for adjusting to a different culture and lifestyle.

CHAPTER FOURTEEN

FINDING YOUR WAY, LIVING YOUR DREAMS

- Building Your Self-Esteem

- Seven Ways to Build Your Self-Esteem

- How Do I Choose a Career?

- I'll Never Use That in Real Life

- It Starts With a Dream: Goal Setting

- Busting Dream Busters

Did you know?

The human brain cell can hold 5 times as much information as the Encyclopedia Britannica.

BUILDING YOUR SELF-ESTEEM

The student years can be very difficult. Peer pressure, drugs, sexuality, bullying and family matters are just a few of the issues that impact the way you may feel about who you are.

Yes, it can be overwhelming to deal with all of the above and still concentrate on school and a job. However, the quicker you learn to build your self-esteem the easier it will be to address most of the above issues.

Where do you start? If asked, many of you will probably say you have high self-esteem. Nonetheless, we'll explore further and help you not only say you have high self-esteem but actually feel like you do.

EXERCISE

What is self-esteem?

How do you know when you have it?

How do you know when your self-esteem is low?

Can you fake it? How?

How can self-esteem affect your school and work performance?

What things, actions, and events can lower your self-esteem?

How do you build up your self-esteem?

Note: Part of building and maintaining your self-esteem is to surround yourself with positive, supportive people. Make sure you have at least one positive adult on whom you can rely.

When you are discouraged, whom can you depend on to lend a listening ear? List their names.

Adults

_____

_____

Peers

_____

_____

SEVEN WAYS TO BUILD YOUR SELF-ESTEEM

1. Do something nice for yourself often.

2. Keep a portfolio with examples of all your successes.

3. Do not beat yourself up when you make mistakes.

4. Find people who believe in you and who will cheer for you always.

5. Set goals.

6. Have a positive attitude.

7. Engage in an activity where you are at your best.

HOW DO I CHOOSE A CAREER?

There are many different careers to choose from. You can be a teacher, a mortician, a computer technician, engineer, and the list goes on. So how do you choose a career? Find a way to do what you enjoy most and get paid for it. That's the secret formula to be successful in life.

Begin your career exploration now. Conduct informational interviews with family, friends or alumni of your school and take part-time jobs in different fields. If you are interested in a particular field but you do not know anyone in the field, get online and identify a company in that field and call their offices to request an informational interview. If your school has a career program, ask your counselor to help you.

EXERCISE

Take a few moments to think about your future and write down your thoughts. Forget about what your friends may think and block out any thoughts that may suggest "I can't do that" or "How am I going to do that?" You can achieve your dreams when you work at it one small piece at a time. Let's get started!

What career do you dream of?

Three reasons why you want this career.

What are the educational requirements for this career?

What do you need to do immediately to make sure you're on the right track?

What skills, characteristics and/or personality traits do you currently have that will help you in your future career?

List at least one action you can take every month that will help you achieve your dream career.

What barriers may prevent you from achieving your dream career?

Who can you turn to for help to break down these barriers and what can you do on your own?

I'LL NEVER USE THAT IN REAL LIFE

Before you start considering your future career, think about the subjects you currently enjoy. Believe it or not, there are lots of careers you can do utilizing the subject you like the most. You may ask, "What on earth can I do with this in real life?" Take a look below.

Math
Sound engineer
Stunt coordinator

English
Journalist
Public relations specialist

Science
Crime scene investigator
Perfume creator

Art
Museum curator
Artist

Vocational Careers
Race car mechanic
Movie set designer
Food stylist
Beautician

IT STARTS WITH A DREAM: GOAL SETTING

Once you take the time to build your self-esteem and decide your career, achieving your dreams becomes a lot easier. We all have dreams. Maybe you dream of becoming an actor, a famous sports star, a teacher or even a doctor. Stretch your imagination to dream of what you want to be when you get older. Think about what kind of lifestyle and career you want. There are absolutely no limits to what you can do once you make the commitment to succeed.

In order to achieve your dreams you must know the following:

1. Everyone who has ever accomplished a dream has overcome obstacles. Do not let the obstacles deter you from dreaming big and going after your heart's desire.

2. You must realize that no one wants to be a failure. Failure to plan and think through the process of achieving a dream often makes dreams fail.

3. Everyone gets help and everyone needs help. Think about the people who can help you: a professor, a family member, an older friend, your supervisor, or a co-worker at your after-school job. Even if you are a bit shy, most adults really do want to help you. It's up to you to be persistent, consistent and ask.

No one becomes successful by sitting around and daydreaming; it takes hard work, determination, consistency, passion, and the will to press on even when things seem impossible.

People who succeed are people who have a plan and act on it consistently and persistently. Those who do not have a plan are really planning to fail.

Dream big, and when you dream know that there are many people waiting for you to take the first step and then they will be there to support you.

EXERCISE

They say goals are dreams with deadlines. When setting goals, you must have a plan and get it down on paper. Make sure that your goals meet goal-setting criteria such as the ones below. This will increase your chances of actually realizing your goals. Use the following pages to write down your goals and record your progress.

Goal-Setting Criteria

1. Set goals that are precise. Be very specific about the goals you want to accomplish.

2. Track and assess your goals. You should be able to measure the progress you are making throughout the process.

3. Make sure you can manage your goals. It makes no sense to set goals if you are not willing to commit yourself to achieving them.

4. Set realistic goals. This does not mean you shouldn't dream big but consider the sacrifices needed to attain your goals.

5. Set a time limit. Your time limit could be two weeks, two months or two years. Whatever you choose, when the time is up you should have accomplished your goals.

You should have goals for different parts of your life. You can set personal, academic and career goals. The most important thing for achieving your goals is to take action on a regular basis to accomplish whatever it is you desire.

PERSONAL GOAL

Goal:

Time limit:

What's the plan of action?

Obstacles encountered?

Possible solutions to resolve obstacles.

People who will listen to you and help you think through your goal.

Five things you can do to stay motivated throughout the process.

Did you achieve your goal on the first attempt?
(See Plan B on next page if you did not achieve your goal)

160

Date goal was accomplished.

Describe how you felt after achieving goal.

New things you learned during this process.

Why Having a Plan B is Important

Sometimes it takes more than one try to achieve a goal. Be open-minded and willing to try different approaches should the first attempt be unsuccessful.

Why didn't plan A work?

What's the new approach?

Possible solutions to resolve obstacles.

People who will listen to you and help you think through your goal.

Things you can do to stay motivated throughout the process.

Date goal was accomplished.

New things you learned during this process.

Describe how you felt after achieving goal.

ACADEMIC GOAL

Goal:

Time limit:

What's the plan of action?

Obstacles encountered?

Possible solutions to resolve obstacles.

People who will listen to you and help you think through your goal.

Five things you can do to stay motivated throughout the process.

Did you achieve your goal on the first attempt?
(See Plan B on next page if you did not achieve your goal)

Date goal was accomplished.

Describe how you felt after achieving goal.

New things you learned during this process.

Why Having a Plan B is Important

Sometimes it takes more than one try to achieve a goal. Be open-minded and willing to try different approaches should the first attempt be unsuccessful.

Why didn't plan A work?

What's the new approach?

Possible solutions to resolve obstacles.

People who will listen to you and help you think through your goal.

Things you can do to stay motivated throughout the process.

Date goal was accomplished.

New things you learned during this process.

Describe how you felt after achieving goal.

CAREER GOAL

Goal:

Time limit:

What's the plan of action?

Obstacles encountered?

Possible solutions to resolve obstacles.

People who will listen to you and help you think through your goal.

Five things you can do to stay motivated throughout the process.

Did you achieve your goal on the first attempt?
(See Plan B on next page if you did not achieve your goal)

Date goal was accomplished.

Describe how you felt after achieving goal.

New things you learned during this process.

Why Having a Plan B is Important

Sometimes it takes more than one try to achieve a goal. Be open-minded and willing to try different approaches should the first attempt be unsuccessful.

Why didn't plan A work?

What's the new approach?

Possible solutions to resolve obstacles.

People who will listen to you and help you think through your goal.

Things you can do to stay motivated throughout the process.

Date goal was accomplished.

New things you learned during this process.

Describe how you felt after achieving your goal.

THINK BIG

DREAM BIG

BELIEVE IN YOURSELF

"You must begin to think of yourself as becoming the person you want to be." **David Viscott**

BUSTING DREAM BUSTERS

There are lots of distractions that can cause setbacks for future careers. Attitude problems, teen pregnancy, drug abuse, hanging out with the wrong people, a boyfriend or girlfriend, violent behavior and/or lack of self-motivation are just some dream busters that can stop or slow down your progress.

What behaviors do you engage in that can possibly destroy your dream or cause a significant setback?

Why do you currently do these things?

Do you see the need to change? Why or why not?

List some of the short-term and long-term consequences of your behavior.

What can you do to change those behaviors?

If friends or family members are hindering your progress, how do you plan to handle them?

Note: Whenever you decide to change, there will be moments when you are not motivated to continue to move forward. You need a plan to pull you out of those moments so that they're not prolonged.

When you get discouraged, what will you do to maintain your new positive way of life?

Who can you trust to talk to about your feelings?
(Make sure you have a trusted adult who can offer sound guidance.)

CHAPTER FIFTEEN

MANAGING CAREER LANDMINES

- Five Forbidden Sins on the Job

- The Impact of Overly Involved Parents

- Rebounding After Juvenile Hall and Jail

- Love's Negative Impact On College, Your Job and Your Life

- Eight Reasons Office Romances Do Not Work

- The Right Way to Quit a Job

- The Office Party, Summer Picnics, Luncheons and More

- Six Ways to Cope with Pressure

- Eight Ways to Relieve Stress

Did you know?

Sixty-two percent of Americans say work has a significant impact on stress levels.

FIVE FORBIDDEN SINS ON THE JOB

1. Drug usage of any kind on the job or coming to work under the influence of any substance is absolutely unacceptable.

2. Dating someone on the job is not professional. It can jeopardize your job if the relationship does not work out. It can also cause tension among co-workers when the relationship seems to be going well.

3. Stealing money or company property is a criminal offense and you can be prosecuted.

4. Cheating on your time card, whether it's adding 10 minutes or an hour, is still cheating and you can be asked to leave.

5. Weapons of any kind are not allowed on company property.

THE IMPACT OF OVERLY INVOLVED PARENTS

Parenting has changed over the last 20+ years, and some parents of young adults are very involved in their lives. Having a strong supportive family is essential in the growth and development of a young person but at some point that individual must learn how to be more self-sufficient. Gabriel Ramos Diaz put it best when he said, "You raise children until they are about 10 years, then you allow them to steer their own ship and you become an advisor." Parents are not advisors if they...

- Call to let your job know you will be out sick when you are not gravely ill.
- Check with your manager/supervisor to ask how you are doing on the job.
- Come to your job interview to evaluate the work environment.
- Research the companies and positions where you should apply and hand you the list.
- Complain to hiring managers if you are not chosen for a position.
- Negotiate your job offer for you.
- Write your résumé and cover letter for you with little or no input from you.
- Call your college professors to ask about your attendance record in classes and if you are completing assignments.
- Write your college papers for you.

A good parent advisor for an adult child will allow you to do all of the above on your own but will give you the information so you can make a decision and support you throughout the process. *You do the work!*

Implications of Overly Involved Parents

Although some companies inundated with parental requests have chosen to incorporate parents in recruitment campaigns and social and community service, that is an exception rather than the rule. Many companies are actually annoyed by parents wanting to be actively involved in their adult child's employment.

As a young adult, you must learn to be independent. Yes, consult your parents for guidance but you do the majority of the work and learn to advocate for yourself. Your credibility as an employee is undermined when your parents speak for you. How can an employer trust you to perform at your best and promote you on your own merit if your parents are hovering over your every move? You are smart, capable and completely able. Life is about the journey of developing and growing each and every day. You will make mistakes—it's part of the journey—but you are supposed to get better and rebound from those lessons each and every time. The older you get the more self-sufficient you are expected to be.

REBOUNDING AFTER
JUVENILE HALL AND JAIL

Have you already made a decision that landed you in juvenile hall or even prison? Most companies and colleges don't really care why you were there. They just know that you spent time in a correctional facility and that makes them apprehensive to consider you as a serious job applicant or potential college student.

Some people do learn skills while behind bars that they hope will be useful when they get out, but they still need to overcome that stigma of being a court-involved youth. Let's look at what can be expected in the world of work and how to handle some of those obstacles when re-entering society.

Go back to school. If you do not have your high school diploma, make every effort to get it but don't stop there. Seriously consider pursuing a trade certificate or a college degree. This will increase your earning power and expose you to positive environments where you can grow.

Put a résumé together. If you had work experience prior to incarceration, pull a résumé together and begin knocking on doors. Be honest when completing applications and attending interviews. Don't lie about your background because it *will* eventually catch up with you.

Career limitations. It's a fact that your record may exclude you from certain careers. Careers in law enforcement, certain financial careers and federal jobs may be out of reach if you have a criminal background.

Don't get too picky. If you can get your foot in *any* door, take the job as long as it is legal — regardless of what it is or how much it pays. Once you prove yourself, you can always work your way up or move on. You will have to demonstrate that you can actually hold a job and be a responsible worker.

Don't give up. Expect many employers and colleges to say "no" to you, but hold onto the hope that you'll find that one person who is willing to offer you an opportunity. Don't get bitter or discouraged. Keep pushing — you *will* find an opportunity.

Consider self-employment. If you picked up a few skills while you were in detention or have prior experience, try your hand at a small entrepreneurial venture. You will need to start small with a venture that does not require a lot of capital, or borrow money from friends and family as most banks will be reluctant to lend you any funds.

Stay clean. Disassociate yourself from the people and habits that landed you in the detention center in the first place; otherwise, you are headed right back as those bad habits will eventually catch up with you. Find new people who will support your clean, legal way of life.

LOVE'S NEGATIVE IMPACT ON COLLEGE, YOUR JOB AND YOUR LIFE

Each year young people fall in love, and each year there are stories of young people who allow what they thought was love to destroy promising lives and opportunities.

Story 1

V was a straight-A student with a full scholarship at a prestigious university and an internship at a company where she loved learning about her dream job. She was so good that the company encouraged her to stay in school and hinted at a full-time position when she finished school. She had already been full time the last two summers. She encountered some problems at home and turned to her new boyfriend for help. He was a high-school dropout with a good job as a welder who dabbled with a little marijuana. Within 6 months V began missing days at school, failed to graduate her senior year, lost her job, and was now a college dropout with a baby on the way.

Story 2

C was a college student with the opportunity of a lifetime to travel abroad with her school on a special summer trip. It would mean she would be away from her boyfriend and they were planning on being engaged in a few years. He objected and she turned down the opportunity. Two months later the relationship fell apart. C regrets turning down the opportunity.

Story 3

M was a marginal student and followed all the rules. He was good in sports and very popular. With plans to head off to college, he discovered his girlfriend was pregnant and she was keeping the baby. M soon realized that his dream to attend college would have to wait while he figured out how to earn a living to support his new family.

Story 4

H was very serious about his new love; in fact, he felt this was "the one". He could not stop thinking about his special someone--in class, after school, even during the chemistry exam. He could not believe his luck. His teachers and family noticed that he seemed a little preoccupied, but he did not see it. He was happy for once in his life until the relationship ended less than 5 months later. He thought, "How could this happen?" H isolated himself, and although he never missed classes, he seemed to have lost his zeal for life and living.

Mature love...

— is not a feeling, it is a decision.
— is patient.
— is kind and gentle.
— is not easily angered.
— allows the other person to express themselves.
— gives you room to grow and be yourself.
— respects your family and friends.

Mature love does NOT...

— need sex to express itself.
— exhibit jealousy.
— try to change you.
— be physically abusive.
— check up on you if you don't stay in touch daily.
— threaten you.
— blame you for all the wrong in other people's lives.
— use you as a sex object to fulfill their every sexual desire.
— get serious and committed quickly.
— get angry when you want to end the relationship.
— make fun of you, insult you or embarrass you in public or behind closed doors.
— get in the way of positive future aspirations.

EIGHT REASONS OFFICE ROMANCES
DO NOT WORK

If you are attracted to someone you work with and you act on those feelings, you are setting yourself up for a bad situation. The stakes are just too high. The romance is never just between the two parties where the workplace is concerned. The entire workplace is involved as they often witness the affection and the arguments.

1. In the beginning, the relationship presents a false sense of happiness, excitement and even possible career advancement if a boss is involved. In reality, the majority of workplace romances are often short-lived, empty, and with negative effects on your future career.

2. Romantic involvement often leads to favoritism in assignments, promotions, and schedules, especially when a supervisor and a subordinate are involved. This behavior adds fuel to the fire of low morale among other employees and encourages low productivity and anger in the workplace.

3. It's hard for some workplace lovers to keep their hands to themselves, and many find it exciting to steal a few romantic exchanges when they think no one is looking. This behavior, of course, is unprofessional, and you become a spectacle and an annoyance for your co-workers who are forced to see this behavior.

4. Unfortunately, when workplace relationships go sour, the fallout can be devastating. Your employment is jeopardized and it becomes impossible to work with someone you no longer like.

5. Even though you may remain employed, your reputation in the organization becomes tarnished as you're now the butt of many jokes and juicy material for the gossip circles.

6. It's not unheard of for families to be destroyed in the process as some workplace romances occur between people who are already committed to other people or even married with children.

7. If you truly value your career and your partner, then consider limiting your interaction to outside the workplace. The rule of thumb is dating on the job is never a good idea so avoid it.

8. Strive to be respected always for your contribution to the company, enthusiasm for the job, the skills and talents you possess and your ability to bring out the best in others as it pertains to their job. These are the selling points that will ultimately yield a career that is productive and long lasting.

THE RIGHT WAY TO QUIT A JOB

It happens. Sometimes a job just is not working out; maybe you've outgrown the job, or you no longer enjoy working with the people, or a better opportunity has come your way. Whatever the reason, it's important to end your relationship with the company the right way. You might need a reference from them sometime.

What's the right way to leave?

It is not acceptable or professional to just go in and say "I quit" and leave, never to return. Although you may feel the company deserves it, that could hurt you later on. The world is a small place, and it pays to end these relationships on a positive note as you may cross paths with some of the same people later on in life.

Keep these rules in mind as you prepare to leave your job.

1. Write a brief letter of resignation, simply stating that you will be resigning from your position and give the date you plan to stop working. Don't mention any problems or complaints. You don't really have to give a reason for leaving!

2. Give your employer at least 2 weeks' notice before you leave the job.

3. Do not take company property with you when you leave, no matter how small. That is considered stealing.

4. Continue to do a good job until your last day and, if asked, be willing to help the new person.

5. No matter why you are leaving, especially if it is under questionable circumstances, never bad mouth anyone in the company or spread gossip about your situation. It is usually safest not to say anything at all.

THE OFFICE PARTY, SUMMER PICNICS, LUNCHEONS AND MORE...

It's not uncommon for companies to roll out the welcome mat for interns and new hires. Summer picnics, luncheons, boat cruises and even professional sporting functions can all be a part of the experience. But it's all a game and here are some of the rules.

It's not really a party. It's a business meeting, and all the professionalism of office behavior is still expected. This includes the annual holiday party.

You are being watched. Many of these social gatherings serve as an opportunity for senior level decision makers to observe how you handle yourself in certain settings. Do you exhibit behavior that can be a liability to the company's reputation or your career?

Stay away from the alcohol. Even if your boss and colleagues are consuming alcohol and encouraging those over 21 years old to have a drink, keep a clear head and sip on some ginger ale or seltzer water on the rocks.

Brush up on your table manners. There are always award banquets, galas and dinners at work colleagues' homes. If you haven't taken a course in fine dining, do so. This will save you from potentially embarrassing moments that may put at risk any chance of future employment with a particular organization.

Dress for the occasion. You don't want to wear skimpy clothing, even if it's poolside or at the beach. Don't be the guy in the Speedo or the girl in the string bikini just to show off your tanned or well-built body. Dress moderately and appropriately for the occasion.

Avoid texting or checking emails. Immerse yourself in the social event and leave the social networking for after the event. Consider leaving your phone in the car or just turn it off.

SIX WAYS TO COPE WITH PEER PRESSURE

1. Remember that you are unique and believe in yourself.

2. Develop many interests and hobbies to vary the kinds of people you meet.

3. Know that differences are to be celebrated.

4. Get counseling.

5. Develop a talent or skill that will help you get to know yourself better.

6. Begin to define and write down your values and moral beliefs.

EIGHT WAYS TO RELIEVE STRESS

1. Set up an action plan.

2. Stay focused on your goals.

3. Resist negative habits and influences.

4. Develop a spiritual life.

5. Surround yourself with people you want to be like.

6. Decrease stressful environments and people in your life.

7. Re-think your priorities in life.

8. Talk to people you trust (friends, parents, school counselor, religious leader), call a youth helpline, or join a support group.

CHAPTER SIXTEEN

TAPPING INTO YOUR ENTREPRENEURIAL TALENTS

- Be Your Own Boss

- Ten Business Ideas for You

Did you know?

The game Monopoly was created in the 1930s after the Stock Market crash.

BE YOUR OWN BOSS

Sometimes it may not be possible to find a job when you need to and you might want to blaze a new trail. There is a solution — become your own boss!

Some of the world's most successful millionaires today are people who started their own business. Although you may not become a millionaire just because you own a business, there is a wonderful sense of accomplishment to know that you are in charge.

Owning your own business, however, does not come easy. You still have to work just as hard, if not harder, and often work more hours, too. The biggest difference is that you are the boss; you set all the rules and bear all the responsibilities, whether the business does well or it fails.

TEN BUSINESS IDEAS FOR YOU

1. Babysitting. Parents will always need a responsible, reliable person to care for their children. If you enjoy children, then consider taking a first-aid class so you can handle emergencies. Begin to talk to parents in your neighborhood, religious groups, and family friends and let them know you are available.

2. Website Designing. Some young people are very internet savvy. If you are and you enjoy it, use your skills to build sites for small business owners in your neighborhood. Put up a sign about your services but the best way is through word of mouth. Build a site for a friend or family member to showcase your skills, ask for a reference and then spread the word.

3. Computer Instructor. If you are very adept at working with a computer and enjoy sharing your knowledge, you can use these skills to teach the ins and outs of computers to senior citizens and any adults who are still not computer literate.

4. Graphic Designing. If you are a great artist and know how to use different art-based programs, why not offer your services to local religious organizations, camps, and especially small businesses to design their flyers and promotional material.

5. Clowning Around. It may sound funny, but clowns are always wanted at kids' birthday parties and it pays very well. Visit your local costume and joke shops for all the equipment a clown could want, then start advertising with friends and neighbors. The word will spread if you are good. You will need a car or a reliable ride.

6. Catering. If your passion is food, consider making sweets, bottled preserves, and other baked goods for all your friends, family, and parents in the neighborhood. Provide samples so they can see how good you are, then start taking orders for parties and other special occasions. Be sure to adhere to all food health codes in your area.

7. Yard Care. Regardless of where you live geographically, you will have some of the following: snow to shovel, leaves to rake, lawns to mow, and there will always be home owners who would rather hire students to do that work.

8. Creative Crafts. If you are more of a hands-on type person, consider making jewelry or crafts, knitting or embroidery, or creating attractive accessories.

9. Family Assistant. That's a fancy way to say that you can run errands for people who are unable to do their own errands because their schedules are too busy or they are homebound. You can take care of the post office needs, dry cleaning, or even pick up groceries, gifts, or medications.

10. Pet Assistant. Although many people value their pets, they sometimes need help taking care of them. You can offer pet-walking services or even be a pet guardian while the owners are on vacation or on business trips.

CHAPTER SEVENTEEN

JOURNEY OF A THOUSAND MILES

- My Life Collage

- My Journal

MY LIFE COLLAGE

Use these next few pages to create a life collage. Look through magazines and cut out pictures that you would like to see in your life. It could be the picture of the house you hope to live in, the car you want to drive, the career you want, or the college you want to attend. It doesn't matter. This is a visual reminder of what you aspire to be. Look at it daily and let it serve as a motivator for you.

Place Pictures Here

MY JOURNAL

"I have only just a minute, only sixty seconds in it, forced upon me – can't refuse it. Didn't seek it, didn't choose it. I must suffer if I lose it. Give account if I abuse it, Just a tiny little minute-- but eternity is in it." **- Benjamin Mays**

"Dream as if you'll live forever. Live as if you'll die today." - **James Dean**

"There are two educations. One should teach us how to make a living and the other how to live." - **John Adams**

"Men occasionally stumble over the truth, but most of them pick themselves up and hurry off as if nothing had happened." - **Sir Winston Churchill**

_____
_____
_____
_____
_____
_____
_____
_____
_____
_____
_____
_____
_____
_____
_____
_____
_____
_____
_____
_____
_____
_____
_____
_____
_____
_____
_____
_____
_____
_____

"I find that the harder I work, the more luck I seem to have."
*- **Thomas Jefferson***

_____
_____
_____
_____
_____
_____
_____
_____
_____
_____
_____
_____
_____
_____
_____
_____
_____
_____
_____
_____
_____
_____
_____
_____
_____
_____
_____
_____

"Whether you think that you can, or that you can't, you are usually right."
- Henry Ford

"Talent does what it can; genius does what it must." - **Edward George Bulwer-Lytton**

"It's kind of fun to do the impossible." - **Walt Disney**

"Knowledge speaks, but wisdom listens." - **Jimi Hendrix**

"I have often regretted my speech, never my silence." - **Xenocrates**

"Obstacles are those frightful things you see when you take your eyes off your goal." - *Anonymous*

"The secret of success is to know something nobody else knows."
- **Aristotle Onassis**

_____
_____
_____
_____
_____
_____
_____
_____
_____
_____
_____
_____
_____
_____
_____
_____
_____
_____
_____
_____
_____
_____
_____
_____
_____
_____
_____
_____
_____
_____

"Don't take life too serious. You'll never escape it alive anyway."
*- **Elbert Hubbard***

"Only the wisest and the stupidest of men never change." - **Confucius**

"Do not follow where the path may lead. Go instead where there is no path and leave a trail." - **Ralph Waldo Emerson**

"Never forget that only dead fish swim with the stream." - **Malcolm Muggeridge**

_____

_____

_____

_____

_____

_____

_____

_____

_____

_____

_____

_____

_____

_____

_____

_____

_____

_____

_____

_____

_____

_____

_____

_____

_____

_____

"Half the things that people do not succeed in, are through fear of making the attempt." - James Northcote

_____
_____
_____
_____
_____
_____
_____
_____
_____
_____
_____
_____
_____
_____
_____
_____
_____
_____
_____
_____
_____
_____
_____
_____
_____
_____
_____
_____
_____
_____

"The man who fears suffering is suffering from what he fears." - **Anonymous**

"Think of these things, whence you came, where you are going, and to whom you must account." - **Benjamin Franklin**

"Energy and persistence conquer all things." - **Benjamin Franklin**

RESOURCES FOR YOUNG ADULTS

Internhere.com
Internhere.com helps students connect with Connecticut and Massachusetts employers offering great internships.
www.internhere.com

Urban Interns
Urban Interns is a new community that connects prospective interns and job seekers with relevant employers, jobs and internships, and specializes in virtual and part-time work. Interns and job seekers can also peruse the listings to find great internships, jobs and co-working spaces.
www.Urbaninterns.com

City Year
City Year unites young people ages 17-24 of all backgrounds for a year of full-time service, giving them the skills and opportunities to change the world.
www.cityyear.org

Toastmasters International
Toastmasters International is a nonprofit educational organization that operates clubs worldwide for the purpose of helping members improve their communication, public speaking and leadership skills. Through its thousands of member clubs, Toastmasters International offers a program of communication and leadership projects designed to help men and women learn the arts of speaking, listening, and thinking.
www.toastmasters.com

INROADS

The mission of INROADS is to develop and place talented minority youth in business and industry and prepare them for corporate and community leadership. INROADS seeks high-performing students for internship opportunities with some of the nation's largest companies.
www.inroads.org

Job Corps

Job Corps is a free education and training program that helps young people learn a career, earn a high school diploma or GED, and find and keep a good job.
www.jobcorps.gov

Rotary International

Rotary is a worldwide organization of more than 1.2 million business, professional, and community leaders. Members of Rotary clubs, known as Rotarians, provide humanitarian service, encourage high ethical standards in all vocations, and help build goodwill and peace in the world.
www.rotary.org

THE BLACK COLLEGIAN

THE BLACK COLLEGIAN is a career and self-development magazine targeted to African-American students and other students of color seeking information on careers, job opportunities, graduate/professional schools, internships/co-ops, study abroad programs, etc. The magazine is distributed on over 800 campuses nationwide, primarily through the career services office.
www.theblackcollegian.com

National Urban League Young Professionals
The National Urban League Young Professionals (NULYP) is a National Urban League volunteer auxiliary that targets young professionals ages 21-40 to empower their communities and change lives through the Urban League Movement.
www.nul.org

Downtown Women's Club
The Downtown Women's Club (DWC) has evolved into an online and in-person community designed for smart and sophisticated businesswomen on the go. Our mission is to empower women through access to information and opportunities for collaboration.
www.downtownwomensclub.com

NFTE- Network for Teaching Entrepreneurship
The Network for Teaching Entrepreneurship's mission is to provide programs that inspire young people from low-income communities to stay in school, to recognize business opportunities and to plan for successful futures.
www.NFTE.org

Other Books by Karen Hinds

Get Along, Get Ahead:
101 Courtesies for the New Workplace

$15.00
Bulk Rates Available

More than 101 quick, practical ways you can use politeness to position yourself for advancement in your career, ease tension with coworkers, interact with your managers/supervisors better, and give excellent customer service. *Get Along, Get Ahead...*is a must read for anyone who wants to be professional, polished, and personally effective.

Networking for a Better Position and More Profit

$7.99
Bulk Rates Available

This book will help you to build long-term professional relationships, explore the unwritten rules that can strengthen new and existing connections, develop a networking plan, use your expertise to help others, grow your network and identify proven follow-up techniques.

Workplace Success Group LLC

Bring Karen Hinds and her associates to your
organization.

- Global events in colleges, universities and high
  schools

- Corporate training programs

- Monthly mentoring subscriptions

- Books, DVDs and e-learning programs

Contact us

Toll Free: 877-902-2775

International Callers: 203-757-4103

www.workplacesuccess.com

Download the eBook today!

www.workplacesuccess.com